CW01471662

Praise for *You'll Like It When You Get There*

'The millennial David Sedaris, the closest I've had
to stand-up as a reading experience.'
Adam Kay

'Relatable tales of adolescent embarrassment, smart
takes on modern life, and all the laughs you'd expect
from such a talented comedian.'
Stephen Merchant

'Just like his stand up, this book is brilliantly written, funny
and makes me love him a lot. How annoying.'
Aisling Bea

'Hilarious, astute, profound. Make an appointment
to read – and for God's sake keep it.'
Danny Wallace

'As witty and clever as Rhys's stand up, but
you can take it in the bath.'
Sara Pascoe

'God damn Rhys for making me laugh out loud reading a
book – the most annoying thing a person can do. Mega
funny and sneakily wise. Nuanced and hilarious takes
on the decisions facing all 30-somethings.'
Phil Wang

'It's a cry for help, but it's a very funny one.'
Dara Ó Briain

'It turns out Rhys James is not only a brilliant comedian,
he's also a fabulously talented writer. I tore through this
book in one sitting because it's such a total joy to
read – laugh out loud funny and endlessly relatable.'
Emily Dean

You'll Like It When You Get There

A Life Lived Reluctantly

Rhys James

WILDFIRE

First published in 2025 by Wildfire
An imprint of Headline Publishing Group Limited

1

Cataloguing in Publication Data is available from the British Library

Hardback ISBN 978 1 0354 2041 4

Typeset in 13/16.5 pt Sabon MT Pro by Six Red Marbles UK, Thetford, Norfolk

Printed and bound in Great Britain by Clays Ltd, Elcograf S.p.A.

MIX
Paper | Supporting
responsible forestry
FSC® C104740

Headline's policy is to use papers that are natural, renewable and recyclable products and made from wood grown in well-managed forests and other controlled sources. The logging and manufacturing processes are expected to conform to the environmental regulations of the country of origin.

Headline Publishing Group Limited
An Hachette UK Company
Carmelite House
50 Victoria Embankment
London EC4Y 0DZ

The authorised representative in the EEA is Hachette Ireland,
8 Castlecourt Centre, Dublin 15, D15 XTP3, Ireland (email: info@hbgi.ie)

www.headline.co.uk
www.hachette.co.uk

For Gary Jenkins

Contents

Bald Ambition   1
Cease the Day   7
Grin and Bare It   15
'Til Death Do We Have To?   33
But I Am le Tired   47
No Kidding   71
The Jungle VIP   91
Neighbourhood Listen   109
Sex and Other Fears   123
Shrinking Violet   141
Sweet Baby James   159
Based on a True Story   173
To Dare Is to Do   193
The World Is My Oyster Card   213
When Life Gives You Molehills,
Make Mountains   223
Acknowledgements   245

Bald Ambition

I'm at the top of a modest mountain, looking for my trainers in a big pile of Birkenstocks as a Buddhist monk quite forcefully asks me to give his monastery five stars on Tripadvisor. I get it, this is the world we live in, and even monks must adapt. But it does feel quite self-defeating. What happened to accepting yourself? To freeing yourself from the judgement of others? If I give him three stars, is his day ruined? Is all that humming and chanting out the window? Does he rip off his orange robe and smash up the pagoda? He tells me it 'really helps the monastery', like it's a podcast. I half expect him to say 'available wherever you get your inner peace'. Presumably he means it 'helps the monastery' to get more visitors and therefore more business for the temple that celebrates the religion that doesn't believe in material gain. Cool. I'm glad I'm seeing this first-hand, because the image of a monk forlornly refreshing Tripadvisor feels a bit too 'rejected Banksy ideas' for me, along with a 'Sky Sports Shown Here' banner on a church and 'Hygiene Rating: 2' on the side of a hospital.

Half an hour earlier, I was sitting cross-legged on the concrete veranda, taking part in the guided meditation that this monk, with his almost sarcastically hairy shoulders, was leading, during which we had to close our eyes and trust no one would steal our Nike GORE-TEX at the door. It was still a few months before the monastery opened to the public, and

I'd been granted early access by virtue of the Airbnb I was staying in being run by this monk's mate. I wasn't the only one here – with me were a Dutch couple in their late twenties wearing hiking gear; an incredibly size-mismatched couple from South Africa dressed in the sort of ponchos you see on a sitcom gap-year character; a 60-something Indian woman from Rickmansworth who reminded me of my mum; an athleisure couple who looked like they'd landed directly from Spanish *Love Island* (in which 'Casa Amor' would disgustingly be called 'Love House'). And Daphne, my girlfriend.

Around us, local volunteers were sanding down fifteen-foot white marble statues of the Buddha. Not to be mistaken with 'Budai', who is the fat, bald guy people often have decorative ornaments of, placed on mantelpieces next to their expensive televisions. The Buddha, or Siddhartha Gautama, is the original. He's skinny, wears a hat, and has the most incredible posture you've ever seen. It's no wonder he's less popular as an emblem in the Western world. Not only does the fat, jolly Buddha look a lot more like one of us (picture a Newcastle fan), and not only does he seem objectively like a bit of a laugh (he is often referred to as 'the laughing Buddha'), his sense of enlightenment is a lot more realistic. Of course you'd accept yourself if you had washboard abs and a perfectly straight spine! Of course you'd free yourself from external influence if you looked like an influencer! The original Buddha is impossible to relate to. Fat Buddha has got there in spite of himself. He's still laughing and smiling in the face of what must be some pretty intense bullying. That's true enlightenment. He feels real.

Our guide, the Five Star Monk, bashed out some chanting asking the spirits to grant people freedom from jealousy, anger, bitterness and hatred, starting with the ragtag bunch in front of him, before extending it to our families, then all the people in the country, the world and finally the solar system. So not to worry, Tim Peake, you're covered too. After this, he invited us to sit in contemplative silence for a bit, and despite being cross-legged and barefoot on the hard concrete, the gentle breeze made it quite difficult not to drift off to sleep. He reminded us to use the silence to reflect on the idea of the naked soul, how it is born pure, and negative emotions are merely learned. I came up with two panel show ideas.

When he eventually invited us to open our eyes, I was half expecting him to be wearing a different outfit and for us all to be in a different location, like an Ant and Dec prank. But nothing had changed. Just a bit of leg cramp and a growing urge to phone my agent about my new formats. The monk went around the group, asking which bit of his meditation school we liked best, which should've been the first warning he was a bit too obsessed with feedback. When he got to me, I said I preferred the silence as it gave me a chance to access thoughts and feelings I wouldn't normally have enough time to. What I didn't tell him was that I'd manifested a seven-figure bank balance off the success of *Quids In*, the *Taskmaster* replacement Dave have been crying out for. The monk responded to my selection by joking that I must've disliked his singing voice, and I replied by suggesting he wouldn't get through to judges' houses, which got about as good a laugh as I could ever hope for from a crowd in a post-meditative state. The monk looked crestfallen, even though I suspected he didn't know what 'judges' houses' even meant. Come on, mate, it was your joke to begin with! You tee 'em up, I knock 'em down. It's a bit of fun. I couldn't quite believe I was having to teach a monk that he's too reliant on the opinions of others for his own self-worth, but here we are. Quick, self-enlighten! *Self-enlighten!*

We continued round the circle until my sixty-year-old Indian holiday mum said she too preferred the silence, that the chanting and mantras didn't do anything for her, because she already lives a life free of rage and jealousy.

I cannot begin to tell you how jealous I was to hear that and how angry it made me.

A life free of jealousy? With no anger? Then what are you doing here at a monastery? You've already completed it all! Have you come here to gloat? Can't you see the rest of us are broken? Even the monk is fishing for compliments so he can show off to his monk rivals! Read the veranda.

I'm suspicious, however, that this isn't really the case. Mrs Rickmansworth is not free of jealousy, or rage. She's full of fucking shit is what she is. Of course she *thinks* she's free of those things. She's on holiday. Who's livid on holiday? In 28 degrees with a Fanta Limón, a Maxibon and so little 4G you can't even look at your emails out of habit? I use up all my stress on the journey *to* the holiday. British Airways exists exclusively to drain you of all your inner rage so you arrive with no energy to do anything but chill out for once. It's a good business model and one I'd be more than happy to grant the full five stars.

But get back home, Temporary Mum, and see if you don't feel these things again. Get to Rickmansworth train station, where someone's decided to obliviously tie their shoelace directly on the other side of the ticket barrier, as if they are the only person in the world, and then tell me you don't feel rage! Open Instagram to discover that another comedian, who you know for a fact has never had a single original thought in their life, has been given a BBC pilot, and tell me you're not jealous! Back to reality, bucko. The real world is a cacophony of envy, hatred and bitterness. It's in our nature. We're cave-people trying to survive at the cost of anything and anyone. Life is a Tough Mudder of emotion you didn't even want to take part in and the 28-year-old Dutch couple next to you are the only ones dressed for it.

All my life I've swelled with emotions like rage, envy, fear, melancholia, angst. Sure, I've had my share of elation, pride, love, ecstasy. But it's those negatives that steal focus, that weigh me down, that must be overcome. The ones I always tell myself can be conquered – if I delete my socials, move to Asia, shave my head, find spirituality. If I could just do those things, I could finally be free.

So as I stand on this mountain, watching a monk type the name of his monastery into my phone and peer over my shoulder to check I'm giving him his precious review, I know once and for all that it's all bollocks. It's all a mirage. We will never be free. The human experience is an endless road to approval and we're all Uber drivers trying to up our rating. And you can have that one for nothing, Banksy, if you're reading this.

Cease the Day

Ever since I was a kid, I've been an absolute pussy, filled with dread at the prospect of having to do almost anything. School was the main one, obviously. I once missed forty-four days of a single school year, which is almost a quarter of it, with no serious illness except a case of the Mondays every day. Or 'chronic dread', you might call it. 'You'll like it when you get there' was my mum's favourite line, which usually turned out to be true. (Although she's less smug these days when I say it back to her about retirement homes.) It didn't matter that it was true. That wasn't the point. It was also true of all my other obligations: parties, sport, Beavers. It didn't stop me pretending to be ill to get out of those things too. And this – it may surprise you to hear about a professional stand-up comedian – has not at all left me. I dread most things in my life, most of the time. From the genuinely tedious to the objectively fun. I simply know, as an adult, I have to actually do those things anyway or my life will be considerably more tragic. Good job I kept my Beavers uniform.

When you're younger this is dismissed as shyness, which is far too gentle a term to be taken seriously. I can't tell you quite how alarmed the sentence 'Rhys, come downstairs and say hello' made me, as I'd trudge slowly down from the sanctuary of my bedroom, as if to the pits of hell, to be paraded in front of other adults like some prize-winning whippet. 'Such shiny hair, what healthy teeth,' I imagined them commenting, while in reality asking about my PlayStation or kindly pretending I'd grown. I hadn't. My mum marked our heights on the kitchen door frame every six months, and mine stayed the same for so long, visitors assumed I had died. When I said very little, they'd excuse me as 'just shy', as opposed to 'not at all interested in some forty-year-old called Graham with red wine lips'. Shyness is always seen as something you'll grow out of, but really it's something you shrink into. Why would a kid have a natural disposition of shyness? They're pure and fresh, everything is exciting and everyone's excited to see them. It's why the default kid is a show-off. 'Look at me! Watch this! Oh, you're busy having a conversation with another grown-up? Well, guess what, I've been sick. That'll teach you.' I took the opposite stance. Nervous about all life had to offer because I hadn't done it before and didn't know how it would go. Scared I would find it hard, get it wrong, feel embarrassed, but without the language to express my trepidation, nor the dexterity of burden-lifting excuses that come with age and experience.

We didn't have the vocabulary for this stuff that we do today. If a phrase like 'social battery' existed when I was a child, I probably still wouldn't have had the confidence to use it. But at least people would've understood. Instead, I was left to make up bogus reasons to avoid interactions, like feigning injury to get out of dancing at a wedding. Five years old, wearing the sort of oversized tucked-in Oxford shirt popularised by a young Jerry Seinfeld, in a hotel function room on an island off the coast of Greece, I bravely decided to step onto the dance floor. Big mistake. If you're a cute child at a wedding, every 30-something woman will stumble over to grab both of your hands and yank you around, like a pissed aunt at Christmas dancing with their dog.

After what felt like a lifetime of appeasing these mad old Greek women long after my social battery had depleted, a red-haired lady named Rebecca approached, desperate for a piece of the action. If only I'd had the words for it then. 'Listen, love, I am a child. I should be skidding across this dance floor on my knees, running between the legs of wobbly grandads, sulking in the corner when I'm not allowed a third slice of cake. I should not have to slow dance with you, a strange old lady, to satisfy some sort of mad mummy fantasy you've burdened me with.' But, egged on by every adult in sight, I fulfilled our dance like a duty. I imagine she saw it the same way. As some sort of noble exercise to get the kid involved in the grown-up activities. Both of us in a tango with public perception, thinking we were doing the other one a favour. But for me, the Orangina had already worn off, and I suddenly felt hideously aware of myself, unable to relax into the charade.

So I did what any self-respecting little boy would do, and I faked a foot injury to get out of it. There's an unmistakable look in someone's eyes when they know you're lying but they're deciding to humour you. And that's what was staring back at me as Rebecca aided my mother in applying needless plasters to my completely undamaged heels while I fake-winced in pain that I didn't feel. At least not physically. Most people think stand-up comedians were the sort of kids who demanded attention, twirling for their parents' friends at every opportunity. I just wanted to be left alone. My first words were, 'Back to bed.'

These days, I am armed with a thousand more sophisticated get-out excuses, from the basic, to the nuclear, rising in extremity based on how late I've left it, and how angry I think the person will be. There are mainstays, like diarrhoea, which no one wants to be around. Though you do have to use this sparingly or friends start showing genuine concern for your bowel health – or worse, telling you they don't mind.

Covid is the gift that keeps on giving, and I was sure to take photos of a positive test on several different surfaces the one time I caught it to keep the excuse evergreen.

On the more drastic side, when you need something sudden, nothing much beats the claim that you've sliced into your thumb while chopping vegetables and need to go to A&E. It's not so dramatic it would garner an unethical amount of sympathy, nor interesting enough to be shared with anyone else as gossip. It's also small enough to have likely 'healed' by the time you see them next, especially as it didn't actually happen. If you pop a plaster over the area, it really sells the idea, a trick I learned when I was five. You're going to want to avoid anything much bigger in terms of ailment: there's nothing worse than finding yourself searching 'neck brace' on Amazon. A sliced digit is the perfect sudden catastrophe to get you out of a gig you don't want to do, and though I've never actually used it myself, it's entered my mind on countless occasions when I've reluctantly plodded off to the tube, forcing myself to go out and live my childhood dream. Imagine the look on my face, then, when a comedy promoter recently told me of the refund fiasco they'd been through when their big headline act had pulled out at the last minute due to 'slicing their thumb while chopping vegetables'. Absolutely no chance, pal. Oldest trick in the book.

This is what comedians are really like. It's all relative, of course, and the industry is not without its extroverts. But every time I've been at an industry party, where musicians and actors are also in attendance, what forms, without fail, is Comedians' Corner. Away from the din of the other show-offs. Hidden from the crowd. A few like-minded individuals flocking together, to slag everyone else off quietly, in the safety of familiarity.

This is why I've shied away from discussing this feeling until now. Typically, when someone confesses to this sort of thing, they say they've always thought it was 'just them' who felt this way, relieved to discover there are kindred spirits out there. But I've always assumed how I feel is how everyone feels. No one wants to do anything, surely? No one actually wants to meet anyone new, or have any new experiences? We do it because we have to in order to survive, right? Like eating broccoli, or getting out of bed. Everyone already knows that most things aren't worth doing, don't they? That most parties are rubbish, most films are clunky, most galleries are a waste of money, most books are too long, most people are twats and most conversations are boring? Surely people realise it's far better to do nothing? Delicious, safe, expectation-free nothing. Think about it. What is there to write home about? Nothing. What is whispered in a lover's ear? Sweet nothings. I mean, what else could there possibly be Much Ado About? Thanks, Shakespeare. Thanks for *Nothing*.

But apparently not. I am not claiming my dread is exceptional, simply that it isn't the absolute default, like I assumed. Some people like things. Some people want to leave the house and experience life. Not everyone is attending things in spite of themselves, having to revise the excuses they gave for not coming last time, in case someone asks how their thumb is healing. Not everyone is fifteen minutes late because they were rifling through their wardrobe for a neck brace.

On paper, I think I might have the perfect life. I am a healthy 34-year-old in a long-term relationship, with no kids. I also have two wonderful living parents, two hilarious nieces, a house, an affectionate cat, disposable income, zero responsibilities and a great deal of time on my hands. So why am I not using any of it? This is surely it! This is what it's all about. I should know everything there is to know about wine, or have travelled the entire world, or be some sort of live-music connoisseur. I should be known for my incredible parties. I should be able to tell you all the best pizza places in New York and show you where all the secret cocktail bars in Soho are. They should greet me by name in private members' clubs. Artisan sandwich shops should say 'The usual?' when I enter. I should be living. Seth Rogen and his partner don't have kids and he has a pottery Instagram on which he makes cool vases and ashtrays while smoking *drugs*. Why don't I have a big art studio? Or a prize-winning allotment? Why don't I smoke drugs? Surely by now I should have learned how to make roulade or speak Italian. At the very least, I should have come up with a valid reason for not having done any of those things. I haven't even done that.

I'm well aware there are 'Diems' I should be 'Carpe'ing. There's a reason there's no Latin phrase for 'just sit there', and it would certainly have made *Dead Poets Society* a tougher sell if there was. I also know from experience that 'Just Sitting There'™ too many days in a row is a one-way ticket to depression. I learned this as a child, perfected it during lockdown, and occasionally find myself slipping back into previous form – the daily routine of no routine, the supposed safety of stasis. Meanwhile, my girlfriend is the opposite, seeking out social plans for us both and often having to justify my non-attendance. 'Sorry, Rhys couldn't make it in the end, he's a bit busy *sedens ibi sicut* . . . Yeah, it's a Latin phrase, it means "just sitting there".'

The thing is, you are not allowed to be shy as an adult. You have to 'man up' and get on with it. This is because shyness is intrinsically infantilising. We can't help but associate it with kids. If I said, 'I can't come, I'm shy,' it would be met with laughter, and rightly so – that is objectively funny. It conjures an image of me hiding behind my dad's leg, despite being the same height as him. You might as well say, 'Sorry, Rhys can't make it tonight, he has nits.' You're never going to be taken seriously as a shy person, because it's something you should've gotten over by now. That's why we invented terms like 'social anxiety', so that adults can carry on feeling it without being thought of as childish. We should rebrand nits as 'scalp-itis' while we're at it.

Once I'm actually at anything, I'm fine. You would never be able to tell I have social anxiety if you were social with me, because it's gone by that point. I like it when I get there. My issue isn't the doing, it's the thinking about doing. Dread is my commute. But far too often, it stops me making the journey. I *know* my heel isn't bleeding, but I still can't rip off the plaster.

So how does this attitude chime with being a professional stand-up comedian? How can the person described above possibly subject themselves to a job in which everyone in the room is facing them, waiting for them to speak? And how can this actually be this person's favourite thing to do?

The dread has not gone away. I did my first gig aged seventeen, and seventeen years on I still hope every single gig gets miraculously cancelled right up until the second I step onto the stage, and sometimes even ten minutes after that. I spent years praying the venue would set on fire before every single show, until finally at Montreal's Just For Laughs festival, seconds before the biggest gig of my life, it did. As we all gathered outside, watching as eight fire engines arrived at the theatre, the disappointment from my colleagues was palpable. They audibly lamented such a wonderful opportunity crumbling to ash in front of them. Meanwhile, I was high on pure relief. Who cared if my future career had taken a hit? I no longer had to do a daunting task *right now*. Isn't that what 'living in the moment' is? All the other comedians told me they'd never seen me so 'chipper', and it was hard to deny. I had literally just returned from the shop with champagne.

This book is not a memoir. I am not qualified to write one. Memoirs are for people who have done things. Not for people who actively avoid doing anything. They are for people who make things happen. Not for people who have things happen to them. They're for the active, not the passive. This is a collection of essays and stories. A guide to living a life in shackles of your own making. An exploration of how my angst manifests in real-world situations, and my attempts to overcome it, live with it and use it to my advantage. This is the introvert's manifesto. The overthinker's dossier. The diary of a wimpy kid.

If you've ever celebrated plans being cancelled with an Andy Murray fist pump, secretly prayed for another lockdown, lied about having seen a film just to fit in, attempted to start your own nickname, and tried – in vain – to control the outcome of everything you do, then welcome to the club. We close early, obviously.

Admittedly, I'm not exactly qualified to be a guide either. Most guides aren't. But hopefully we can still learn a few things together regardless, on this deep-dive into the shy-boy psyche. The journey might be rocky, but it's one I hope you'll join me on. So bon voyage, and see you on the other side. Maybe you'll even like it when you get there.

Grin and Bare It

When we first met, I told Daphne that I was immune to embarrassment. Now twelve years older, I know that wasn't true, because I'm embarrassed I even said that. My feeling at the time was that as a comedian, every awful, humiliating thing that happens in my life is ammo. Some would call it material, but as the metaphor for doing well at a comedy gig is 'killing', I think ammo is much more appropriate. Ammo. It's ammo. Is there some deep-rooted toxic masculinity at the heart of this word selection? No way, bitch. Back then, I saw my entire life as ammo. Not just humiliating experiences, but all experiences, all observations, all thoughts. It was all something to potentially speak about during the only thing I ever did: stand-up comedy. I wasn't a person between the ages of eighteen and twenty-six (henceforth to be referred to as 'the railcard years'). I was nothing but a comedian. And comedians aren't people.

A big reason for this naive perspective is that, in my pre-railcard years, when I was still a person, I was defined by embarrassment. Influenced by its ever-looming presence and driven by an overwhelming desire to avoid it. It might be hard to believe, given I used to perform little skits with my friends in end-of-year assemblies and started doing stand-up comedy at seventeen, effectively putting a big sign on my front lawn saying, 'Humiliation, please stop here,' but I saw performing,

and specifically stand-up, as a way to get a hold of my humiliation, to control the narrative by taking ownership of it. Most
would see this as a high-risk strategy. In order to avoid embarrassment, you're going to put yourself in a situation that, if it
goes badly, is without a doubt the most embarrassing experience possible? Absolutely. Big problems need bigger solutions.
Evel Knievel doesn't *want* to crash-land into a row of buses.
He *could* drive his motorbike *around* the buses, but where's
the fun in that? Where's the jeopardy? No – avoid the buses by
trying to jump over them, even though if you fail, everyone
will find it *really embarrassing* – plus several other enormous
consequences. The truth is, a performance that's going badly
doesn't feel embarrassing when you're the one performing. It's
far more embarrassing to watch. It's painful as a performer,
it's awkward, but it's not humiliating. No one did anything to
me. I did something to them. That's the embarrassing part!
I've *put myself out there* and said, 'Look at me, I think I've
got something to offer!' Even if it goes well, that's cringe. But
by the time I'm actually up there? No chance. I'm the one who
got on the bike. The humiliation is in the rear-view mirror. As
long as I don't shit myself in the process, we're golden.

My fear of embarrassment was far more micro. Tiny, insignificant day-to-day things, like not having seen a film
everyone's talking about. That was my main vice in my school
years: pretending to have already done things I hadn't. I
wasn't a bullshitter or a bragger. I lied only in response to
questioning. I wasn't trying to one-up anyone; I was trying to
one-all the world with a late equaliser so they didn't laugh at
me. Every conversation played out the same:

'Sex? Oh yeah, I've done that, literally loads of times. I've
got really quick at it now.'

'Vodka? Big time. Brush my teeth with the stuff. And I

didn't like it, by the way, found it a bit bland actually, so please, PLEASE don't offer me any more. My vodka years are behind me.'

'*Austin Powers*? Of course I've seen it. Bloody bonkers, him.'

Oh, you'd now like to have a conversation about several specific scenes in the film that I couldn't possibly bluff my way through? Well then, I guess it's time I crack my knuckles, performatively stretch and roll out the famous line . . . '*Ah, I've only seen bits of it*. That's right. Bits. Of a *film*. And I suppose the bits I've seen are weirdly none of the ones you're describing. Different bits. That's right, when I went to see this film, which is still only available in cinemas, I would watch for a few minutes at a time and then repeatedly leave the theatre during every significant moment, over and over again, fifty times in ninety minutes, for £12.50. That's just how I watch 'em, I'm afraid. That's how us film buffs do it, so I won't be contributing to this conversation further. Unless you want to talk exclusively about that bit in the trailer where he can't turn his cart around in the narrow hallway? Because I've seen that. Of course I have, I've watched the film. Obviously my parents have said I'm allowed to watch it, so why wouldn't I have? I loved it. The bits of it I saw, that is.'

So deep into this sort of lie was I, that I once asked my best friend Fred if he'd seen turn of the millennium James Bond film *The World Is Not Enough*. He said 'yes' unconvincingly, and having danced this dance myself a thousand times prior, I pushed him on it. 'Oh yeah, what's it about then?' I prodded, like a young Maitlis. 'It's sort of about the world not being enough,' he retorted. I paused, thinking back to the film and its core message. Wow. I couldn't argue. I had been bested. Frankly, Fred had run rings round me with his simplicity.

Checkmate. Right when I had him in my crosshairs, he quickly pulled out his own gun, turned it in my direction and fired straight back. He really did know his Bond. 'Oh, so you have seen it then,' I said, defeated, only to later be reminded of this fable every year at Christmas for the rest of my life.

I was constantly faking things well into adulthood. The same boy who claimed to have grazed heels to get out of dancing with a thirty-year-old redhead at a Greek wedding would find himself, decades later, faking a shoulder injury to get out of having to perform a caber toss on a stag do. It feels so pathetic to write down, knowing that there are no circumstances in which I could participate in the harmless, jovial activity of attempting to throw a big pole of Scottish wood with my closest friends. Why? Because it might be embarrassing? That's the point, Rhys, you moron. It's a stag do. That's what they are designed for. Stag dos, the once quite romantically ironic 'final drink of freedom' the night before a wedding, have descended into these weekend-long medieval public humiliation experiments, where instead of being put in the stocks, the stag is put into a tutu, and instead of having tomatoes thrown at his face, his closest friends concoct a drink lethal enough to kill a small dog before forcing him down onto a chair to be twerked at by an underdressed stranger.

It's only fair, then, that in brief respite for the only person all of us actually know on this somehow culture-less trip to one of Europe's historical behemoths, we share the shame out a little bit. A caber toss, as a stag-do activity, is genius. Failure is almost guaranteed, so it should be constant titters for all. No one here is a caber-tossing expert, and it would be far more embarrassing if they were. And yet there I am, grasping my shoulder like it's suddenly flared up again.

Sometimes this feeling came from a fear of embarrassment, other times from fear in general. I took up skateboarding as a young teenager, but despite making my parents spend a small fortune on all the gear and drive me to an indoor skatepark every Tuesday evening for two years, I never quite plucked up the courage to 'drop in'. For the less gnarly among you, this is the bit in skateboarding when you stand at the top of the halfpipe or ramp and, quite simply, go down it. It's literally how you begin the process of skateboarding. Instead, I would stand sidelined at the top of the ramp, in my spotless Etnies trainers, leaning on my pristine skateboard like a character in Tony Hawk's Pro Skater before you've selected them.

This sort of fear didn't wane with age, still looming large at nineteen, as I sat in the pub with the lads from school during a university break, planning a visit to Sheffield for our friend's birthday. Fred suggested it might be quaint to purchase some Class A drugs for our jaunt, and wanted an idea of numbers. Everyone was excited. Despite the rest of us having been at university a year already while he had stayed home, Fred was the only one among us who had done said drug, so naturally what followed was an excitable if edgy Q&A from the group. My friends' nerves manifested in some light research followed by the gleeful anticipation of trying something new together, the safety in numbers of going through a rite of passage with your most trusted cohorts. How did I respond? I pretended that I had already done this particular drug too much at uni and I'd skip it this time, as it 'didn't agree with me'. Even if that had been in any way true, the entire point of drugs is to not agree with you. The aim is to alter something, whether to distort your interpretation of your surroundings, relax you or, in this case, boost your energy and the pace at which you can talk about how great you are. I mean, if anything, if this drug were a person, it absolutely *would* agree with you, especially if you were suggesting business ideas.

By this point, my friends were pretty familiar with my penchant for caution, or as they called it, 'pussing out', so paid little mind to my tiny personal protest. One of them humoured me, politely asking what it does to me that's so disagreeable. I erroneously claimed it made me 'a bit too paranoid' despite all anecdotal evidence that this drug does the exact opposite (I might as well have said it gives me a blocked nose) and they all quickly moved on to the logistics. I realise now, the fact they didn't push me on it further meant that not a single one of them believed my story, and having watched me flounder under the interrogation lights in the past, decided to spare me.

Fast-forward a few weeks to the big day, and now, with the magic of Dutch courage, and having witnessed all my friends give it a go with no instant consequences, I decide I want in. I'm allowed, with a roll of the eyes at the fact I hadn't contributed financially, and I have a similar issue-free experience to my friends. But it's hollow. I've already missed out on the fun of the whole thing: the anticipation, the collective fear, the geeing each other up, the confronting of a coming-of-age milestone together. All because I let my own fear of the situation get the better of me and force me to save face. I look back on these sorts of tiny moments with such regret, that I couldn't be open and have an honest experience with my friends, instead opting to place myself above it all. 'Oh, your first time, is it? Oh dear. I've already experienced all your future experiences, and by the way, they're rubbish.' It's no life.

To share in something scary together, to get through the other side, to learn something as a collective. That is friendship.

And that's what it cost me. All it cost everyone else was twenty-five quid a head. Which would've been closer to twenty quid if I'd said yes to begin with.

It's a conscious effort these days to open myself up and remind myself that everything was at one point the first time I tried it, and for the most part, turned out fine. But saving face is still a major instinct for me, and one that really isn't becoming for a comedian, who literally trades in monetisable shame. For me, this manifests day-to-day in microcosms. If someone uses a word that I don't know the meaning of, for example, I will never ask what it means, even if it's vital to understanding the sentence. I'll bluff, like always, listing possible synonyms to their word while agreeing and following their frown or smile like 'hotter' or 'colder' clues. Sometimes I'll go so far as to use the word myself, even if I'm using it facetiously, or whatever. The reality is, I'm jealous of the people who do ask, who know that curiosity is a virtue. When anyone asks me to explain anything, I am thrilled to get the opportunity to feel like an expert for a moment and watch someone learn something new first-hand. So it frustrates me no end that I can't let myself be that person, when I know that person is someone everyone appreciates. It's another example of my brain's logic and rationale being at logger-heads with my emotions and instincts, and I find it absolutely salacious.

As I've gotten older, I've realised the people who shame-lessly ask for clarity are a tiny minority, especially in Britain. We are a nation of face-savers, of David Brents, desperately trying to style everything out, claiming, 'Yeah that's what I'm saying,' when proven wrong, pushing out our 'resignation tended by mutual consent' press releases after a brutal sacking. Constantly saying, 'I meant to do that,' and praying our bogus claims don't go to VAR. So many of us immediately look to blame our failings on someone else, while simultaneously sharing self-help podcast clips to our Instagram stories that say, 'It's not about how many times you fall; it's about how many times you pick yourself up.' We like to think we can handle cringe more than Americans, but it's not from any immunity to humiliation, it's from the desperate gratitude that the humiliation is happening to someone else. Listen to how quickly an audience clap when a magician picks a volunteer from the audience. They're not clapping for the individual, but from relief it's someone, *anyone*, other than themselves. The purpose of the applause is to seal the deal. 'There's no backing out of it now, buddy, we've all clapped for you, you wouldn't want us to have clapped for nothing, would you? That's a contract, now get up there and stop Derren Brown throwing his dreaded frisbee in my direction for another fifteen minutes.' When Band Aid sang, 'Well, tonight, thank God, it's them instead of you,' they weren't talking crudely about African poverty, they were referring to audience participation.

Brits literally *celebrate* humiliation, purely because it's happening to someone else. Whether it's an underperforming football team, a mugged-off stag-do attendee, a delusional *Britain's Got Talent* contestant, a 'hacked' celeb accidentally exposing themselves on social media, or someone who has dropped a tray of pints in a pub. 'Wa-hey!' come the jovial cries of the onlookers, but what lies beneath the 'wa-hey' is a deep and visceral 'It's not me! I'm off the hook!' So of course I feel the constant need to save face, I'm British. I dread to think of how many conversations I had with boys throughout my childhood about films neither of us had watched, but both pretended to have seen differing bits of, due to some sort of invisible social shame contract. A force field protecting you from being pointed and laughed at, at the enormous expense of ever making any meaningful connections.

Imagine, then, how it feels for someone this intent on avoiding humiliation and saving face from a young age to experience without a doubt the most stereotypically embarrassing moment possible, at undeniably the most difficult-to-deal-with age, at which peers actually did literally point and laugh.

In every school year, there are three to five boys who are small. The small boys. Smaller than all the other boys, smaller than most of the girls. I don't think it's going to be a major twist to reveal that I was one of them. I can hardly expect book-dropping gasps when my adult brand remains 'little shit'. Sure, these days I am an extremely respectable, significantly above average five foot eleven inches. So secure in fact that I'm not even going to round up to the coveted six foot, but take pride in my five eleven, actually, thank you (having already rounded from five foot ten and a half). But I wouldn't begrudge anyone reading this to secretly harbour the opinion that I do still *seem* small. That's because smallness doesn't leave you, even if you literally outgrow it. Small-boy energy isn't a pencil marking on a door frame or a rollercoaster admissions requirement; it's a feeling in your soul, a look on your face, an attitude you can't mask, that follows you for ever.

There are ways to combat being small at school, of course, and we all fell into line spectacularly. There was Jed, who managed his smallness by being, oh, only the best in the year at football and a butter-wouldn't-melt blond stunner who everyone fancied. Yeah, I think you'll be fine, mate. Christ. Couldn't have shared those attributes out a bit? On the other side of things, you had Stephen, who used his smallness to get into Joe Pesci style capers, setting things on fire and muttering to himself in corners, constantly on the cusp of expulsion, and explosion. Then there were a few dweebs who kept as quiet as possible and spent lunchtimes out of trouble in the library (as most small boys should). And finally me, who went for the A24 version of the story: be really pathetically in love with and overly romantic to every girl smaller than me, before trying on sarcasm and basing my entire personality around witty asides. It was a wisecracker's life for me. Years spent making a constant stream of self-deprecating short jokes that show you're thinking about this a lot more than anyone else gradually moulded into an affected cynicism used to mock everyone and everything. Obviously this wasn't before picking a few popular bigger boys to stand permanently next to for 'protection', the Hammond to their Clarkson. That's the real safe way to combat being short at school: standing on the shoulders of giants, if only to be able to see what's going on.

It wasn't just the height, but the babyface. I was still getting ID'd for paracetamol right up to the pandemic, when the mask covering my cheeky scamp 'shine your shoes, missus' gob and leaving my cold, dead, war-veteran eyes on display put a stop to that once and for all. I was twenty-nine. Until the act of trying to get to the microphone during 'Scenes We'd Like To See' on *Mock the Week* aged me several decades, I think my face was always about five or six years behind my age. How I managed to be let into nightclubs at seventeen with my older brother's provisional driving licence claiming I was twenty, I'll never know, given how much I looked like I was there to clean the chimney. I felt much more at home a few years earlier at the weird children's nightclub they put on during half-term, 'Baby Batchwood'. St Albans, near where I grew up, is home to a golf club called Batchwood which, four times a year, would turn its manor into a sticky-floor, multi-room, noughties R&B nightclub, with cheap VKs and, rather creepily, podiums for teenagers to dance on. I went to every single one. It was here that the combination of my height and babyface manifested into its final form. As all my friends, with their broad rugby shoulders and sprouting facial hair, used these nights to get off with girls, I used them to do silly dances to make girls laugh before they headed off to the seating area with someone who didn't make them look like a nonce. It wasn't even depressing, it was a choice. It was admitting defeat. There was no jeopardy in not looking cool in those moments, because my attempts to look cool would yield no results anyway. It was saving face before it needed saving. I was doing The Worm pre-emptively.

It's no surprise, then, that my mum felt a bit protective of this little boy, adhering strictly to movie age ratings, writing notes to get me out of contact sports in PE, and repeatedly expressing that a single taste of a single drug would kill me on the spot. While I'm grateful for getting to sit out Year 9 rugby, I do sometimes wonder if the drug chat may have had any social consequences for me a few years later, but it's impossible to know.

And I don't blame her. She tried her best to encourage me to do practically everything else. It would've been a bit 'Childline' of her to tell me I'd 'like it when I got there' to the passenger seat of a drug dealer's BMW. Of all the lessons parents learn from their own upbringing and pass down, 'drugs are bad' is probably one of the least toxic. But it's a strange quirk of middle-class boomers that they see drugs as these extremely fatal weapons not to be messed with, despite being completely obsessed with alcohol. A sip of Dad's wine as an adolescent was laughed off as a gentle bit of fun, while a cheeky pill at a concert today is still considered going completely off the rails. Warning someone against the dangers of drugs while knocking back the sort of units per week boomers do is like telling someone to stop smoking while holding a lit firework between your own butt cheeks. Unfortunately, my mum has never really been into booze either, or fireworks, so gets to retain the moral high ground yet again. Why are they always right?

All of this is to say that it had increased significance for me, being a self-conscious late bloomer obsessed with preventing embarrassment, when the aforementioned 'most humiliating thing a person can experience' happened to me at fourteen. I had my pants pulled down in front of my class. Classic.

If my approach to being a small boy was the coming-of-age movie trope, then of course this route-one humiliation cliché was part of the plot. At the vital age when pretty much all anyone talked about was pubes and penis size, and I spent my time masking my inadequacy in both with bravado and condescension, this was the only possible outcome.

On the last day of term, during afternoon registration, I stood up to do an impression of one of our year group when a cheeky outcast called Bobby saw an opportunity to yank down my trendily low-riding trousers, and with the momentum, my boxers followed them to the floor, landing in a heap with my dignity. I had been kegged. 'Pantsed', as they say in America. The reverse wedgie. My secret shame laid bare. So quick was I to cover myself up that the evidence was actually seen by very few, but this was *school*, where gossip spread like chickenpox. And true to the cookie-cutter nature of my teen-movie plot, one of the unlucky viewers just so happened to be the prettiest girl in school, Isabelle.

I wish this wasn't true. I wish I could write something

more original, but this is the truth. I don't need to lie about having watched this movie. I lived it. Ask Isabelle Pritchard if she's ever seen Rhys James. She'll tell you with full confidence: 'I've seen bits of him.'

It doesn't get any more original as it goes on, I'm afraid, even though I responded to my debagging with a psychotic measured silence. In the face of the pointing and laughing I'd so dreaded, I very quietly bent down to pull up my pants, before returning down to my ankles to collect my trousers in a separate action. In hindsight, it feels like I was milking my moment. I walked over to my desk, slowly put on my jacket, picked up my bag and left the school, stopping briefly at the classroom door to turn back and look at my classmates, as though my character in this teen drama was finally moving out of his childhood home and wanted one final look (hand slaps door frame before slowly peeling away, camera pans out on unfurnished living room now full only of memories, 'Closing Time' by Semisonic plays).

Once I got out of the classroom, I raced home in a frantic stumble, like a late tornado. Nothing could get in my way, I had to get out of there. When there's no saving-face left to do, you have to go nuclear and leave the situation entirely. I barged upstairs and paced around my bedroom, lying on my bed to stare unblinking at the ceiling for thirty seconds at a time before pacing around again. My parents were desperate to know what was going on, but I kept quiet, deciding instead to have a full internalised meltdown about how my peers would respond when the bell rang. What will they say? Will people believe it? Are they all going to laugh? Will it be spread with whispers and cruel pinky-finger gestures, or yelled across the playground town-crier style? How will my mates react? Why did I leave? Now I can't deny, or control the narrative. But at least I can't be betrayed by the look on my face. I'm an idiot. I'm a genius. My world was crashing down around me. It was over. Everything I'd built. Everything I'd worked for to combat my smallness. Lost. The smallness beneath had been exposed. The truth had been revealed. My hard-fought identity was evaporating from within. I searched for answers, desperately trying to get a sense of the public response in the pre-social media days of 10p texting. But I didn't want to give anything away in case they didn't know yet. I couldn't type and delete and type again quick enough. I didn't know what to do with myself. I was having a full-blown panic attack. It felt like I was trying to land a hot air balloon in a rush.

And then, suddenly, I knew exactly what to do. It was simple. I had to convince my parents to move. I could never return to that school or see those people ever again. It was over. I had been exiled. Time to start a new life in Bucking-hamshire. Get a new personality while I'm at it. I had until the end of the half-term to get as good at football as Jed.

A week later, I returned to school. Obviously. Metaphor-ical cap in hand. I'd say tail between my legs, but I'd have killed for one of those. I wasn't myself that day. Extremely timid, apprehensive, almost . . . nice. Everyone knew some-thing about me and I walked the halls in nervous anticipation of sideways glances and bitchy whispers. But it was much worse than that. What happened in response was . . . nothing. No one said a word to me about it. Of course they didn't. Like the drug situation in years to come, there was no point. It didn't mean I'd won; it meant it was so embarrassing on its own, it required no further comment. I'd lost twice. How I longed for the group 'wa-hey' of a pub garden, the collective basking in someone's fuck-up because it 'could've been anyone', but this couldn't have been anyone. Dropped pints this was not. Dropped pants were far more serious.

The only communication I ever had on the matter was months later, when I finally was ready to move on. God, bullies are good. It arrived in the form of an email on the school's intranet from one of the main brutes, Laurence. No subject heading. No text in the body of the message. Just a single image attachment. A photo of Condoleezza Rice making a gesture with her index finger and thumb to suggest something was tiny. Once, an indication of shrinking federal budgets from the US Secretary of State. Now, a representation of my adolescent genitals. It's like I was built for topical comedy.

To be honest, this probably tells you more about the sort of school I went to than anything else. That's some pretty sophisticated bullying both intellectually and technologically. After a few days I responded by sending back a similarly wordless email that contained my own image attachment. Condoleezza Rice holding her hands extremely far apart, clearly discussing something enormous. The sort of gesture you'd make to describe a big fish you'd caught. Genius, I thought, before realising in context I'd basically implied Laurence himself had a big knob. All I do is lose.

For years I intellectualised that this moment was my inciting incident to become a comedian. That I must've taken this humiliation and dedicated my life to getting laughs on my own terms instead. I even insisted that I was only capable of doing comedy because of what a thick skin it had given me. That silence in a room full of people I wanted to make laugh was easily preferable to laughter in a room full of people I wanted to be silent. I convinced myself it was a vaccine for embarrassment, giving me complete immunity to ever feeling shame again, even bragging about getting my jab first like a pensioner during lockdown.

Around the time I told Daphne I could no longer feel embarrassment, I was telling my pants-down story on-stage as an early stand-up routine. I now found it funny, obviously, but I also wanted to own it. To package it into something neat and tidy and pop it in the mental storeroom of past events marked 'useful'. To transform it into something productive. Even profitable. To somehow win. When my friends saw my show, they'd mention that routine specifically and ask if it was real. It blew my mind. Real? They were there! They lived through it too! How could they not remember something so seminal? Eventually they'd offer mumbles of vague recognition, but nothing nearly as vivid and visceral as the scenes replaying in my head over and over. It was completely insignificant to them.

Here I was, in a decade-long analysis of something so simple and objectively funny as a teenage boy getting his pants pulled down. Like the tens of thousands of other teenage boys victim to the exact same thing, commonly referred to as 'just a prank, bro'. That's the problem with being introspective. Everything must be rationalised, or rationalise something else. I told myself that a pantsing led to a comedy career which led to the mining of all my shame which led to an immunity to shame itself, to justify one embarrassing moment as completely necessary within the wider Rhys lore. But really, it was a humiliating teenage moment I later got four minutes of stand-up comedy out of, like everything else. Nothing more. Nothing less.

It didn't inspire me to try comedy so I could get laughs on my own terms. I have always been this way. This was the boy who danced for laughs in a nightclub for children and pretended to understand the phrase 'shagadelic, baby'. This wasn't impetus; it was my deepest fear manifesting. My debagging wasn't about awakening something within me. It was about trying to kill something much bigger. It was a Hail Mary from the universe to free me from my plastered-on confidence and force me into a life of authenticity. And when that didn't work, He sent my friends from the future to prove that no one even noticed to begin with. Well, nice try, God, but you can't get me that easily. I've continued doing all I can to save face regardless. I have learned nothing.

Maybe, in another life, in another world, I'll have my penis involuntarily exposed to almost no reaction and it *will* trigger something in me that means I someday feel content to toss the caber and pay my fair share for a gram. But not this life. And not this world. So take that as my message. And if you ever find yourself in the unlikely position that someone asks you what this chapter was about, you can look at them with confidence, and say: 'It's sort of about this world not being enough.'

'Til Death Do We Have To?

It's been suggested that on first dates, people hide their true selves so as to conceal the 'crazy', to make their date fall in love with the more palatable version, waiting to reveal their inner psychopath once it's too late. Despite this, the most common advice on how to approach dating is to 'be yourself'. These seem like conflicting ideas, but I actually think they can be quite easily married together.

When you adopt a kitten and bring it home, you're told to confine it to a single room in your house until it gets comfortable, gradually opening up more and more of the house for the cat to explore. If you let the cat roam from the get-go, it would be far too overwhelming, and while it may look excited, it's going to shit on your sofa. That, I think, is how relationships work. You can still 'be yourself', you just can't be *all* of yourself right away. That would be too overwhelming. Effectively, you're confining a date to a single room (aspect) of your house (personality) so they don't freak out and shit (shit) on your sofa (sofa).

On our first date, my girlfriend told me she hated her job as a part-time nanny of twins, and wanted to someday visit Sri Lanka. I told her I thought royalists were the thickest people on the planet and that I might be bi-curious. I think I may have shat on the sofa.

Really, all anyone wants is to feel understood. To be on a

wavelength with someone. It's not even a conscious feeling, being understood, but not being understood feels so frustrating it works by comparison. Like the sound of a lawnmower you're not even aware of until it switches off, when suddenly you're *so* aware of it, due to its absence. That's what it feels like to have someone finally understand you. Blissful relief. This is why I'll happily get to the real stuff too quickly in conversation, because I know that's who I am, and there's no point having someone understand a fake version of me, pretending to care that you've given up drinking coffee post-2 p.m. and you didn't rate *Slow Horses*.

Being understood is the second greatest thing you can be, right after being fancied. Not loved. Fancied. The feeling of being loved is soft, slow and comforting. It's a constant bubbling, a low simmer. But fancied? That's thrilling. It exists in a moment. It's a flambé. To be loved is to spend three hours driving to the beach. To be fancied is to walk a tightrope over two cliffs. One small slip and it's over.

For a long time I thought being loved was being both fancied and understood at the same time. Now that I've been in a relationship for twelve years I realise it's not that at all. Love isn't understanding; it's the act of *trying* to understand, even when you don't really fancy them very much that day.

My girlfriend is adventurous, social and, above all else, desperate not to be beckoned into the life of nothingness of which I'm the maître d'. She tries to understand my dread; I try to understand her lack of it. She's two years younger than I am and was still at university when we met, but I was immediately blown away by how much more worldly-wise she was than me. I'd sit in the class of Daphne, learning all sorts of things I'd pretend to already know, from the practical to the philosophical, all borne of her innate curiosity that I'd kill to

possess just half of. But all the best couples are this combination. You can't have two extremely outgoing partners, with
their overbearing mutual zest for life and complete lack of
doubt. Who do you think you are – Jedward? But you can't
have two nervous idlers either; they'd complete Netflix in a
week.

This obviously presents its frustrations in our social life.
I'm not the first to observe the phenomenon of 'couple friends',
but for the uninitiated, head to a pub or bowling alley on any
given Friday and observe how the groups of grown-ups you
see are always an even number. Pay attention to the way in
which arms drape across shoulders or hands rest on thighs in
support of each couple's most reluctant attendee. How conversation breaks off into pairs and slowly retreats back again
when the already shallow well quickly runs dry. What you're
observing is couples, often a couple of couples, subtly inter-
viewing each other for the role of couple friends, or in some
more efficient cases, a couple of couple friends at once. These
are friends that can be hung out with as a collective, rather
than bringing your partner along to see your existing mates,
like a plus-one to your past. Couple friends are a fresh start,
and fresh starts are often extremely painful.

Eventually, once the audition process is over and you've
weeded out any couple candidates who may be perverts, or
worse, TikTokers, couple friends are a great thing to have.
Like all relationships, you reach a point where it's comfortable, you're friends with every individual involved, and no
one's pinching you under the table for being too blunt. But
until that happens it's generally the case that your girlfriend
has a friend and that friend has a partner who never organ-
ises anything for them to do, so now you have to sit opposite
him with a Neck Oil and talk about how Arsenal always

drop points in April, while the palpable glee of established chemistry happens right next to you, almost mockingly. As months pass, you level up, reaching such landmarks as 'toiling over which price point is generous without being showy for a bottle of wine you're taking to a dinner party at their flat' all the way up to 'going for a drink with *just* him actually and not as couples' when you realise you haven't texted back any of your actual mates for eighteen months. Ultimately, this is all leading to an invitation to go on holiday together, once one of the couples decides they're ready for you to see them in shorts, during which you'll do nothing but internally compare your relationship dynamics and play Monopoly Deal until the ink stains your fingertips.

While mine and my girlfriend's different personality types might throw up issues with social engagements, thankfully we're in agreement regarding other engagements, such as the engagement of getting engaged. We both don't believe in marriage. Phew. Marriage feels outdated to me. A contract for your relationship. You have no contracts with your friends. If someone wants to stop being friends with you, they just can. You can't say, 'Lawyer up, buddy, I'm taking your Xbox.' But a relationship? No, I'd like employee rights, please, from the person I'm supposed to trust the most in the world. Every proposal is a bet with your partner that they won't love you for ever.

Not to mention the term of such a contract: *'Til death*. You'd accept this from no other contract in your life. Even during a cursory glance over some terms and conditions, the words ''til death' would make you think, 'Maybe I should get a different broadband provider?' The only other thing people sign up to until death is the army, and that's only if something goes wrong. Marriage is until death if it goes well! Surely you need the opportunity to at least renegotiate?

Marriage contracts should be done like footballers' contracts. It'd be a lot simpler if my girlfriend could sign me on a five-year deal, and if I don't stay fit, I have to move to Watford.

People try to sell marriage in a very pragmatic way. Not in quite the same way they try to sell the idea of having kids, in which a friend who looks the absolute worst you've ever seen them tells you how much better their life is now they've been given this magical gift. That sleep is overrated and watching *Frozen* fifteen times a day is a passion project. They grab you by the lapels, desperate and impassioned, and say, 'You don't know what real love is until you have a child,' and I say good, I'll stick with whatever fake love has been keeping my skin so fresh. When they speak to other new parents, their tone is far more realistic, letting out exacerbated sighs and performing dramatic eye-rolls in a bid for camaraderie. But to the childless, it's the full song-and-dance pitch to recruit more members to the cult. Before you have a baby, 'It's the best thing you'll ever do,' but the moment you're having to actually raise one, a pointed tail bursts out of their Frubes-stained dungarees as they usher you into hell.

Marriage is different. No one outside of a cult has ever tried to suggest it's the best thing in the world. Instead, they outline a few practical benefits. 'You get good tax breaks,' they'll say, as if that's enough reason for a lifelong commitment, and they see their partner as a walking ISA. 'We registered in the Cayman Islands.'

Think about what that actually means. The government are effectively going to give you money to get married? And that's supposed to tell me it's good, instead of history's most obvious scam? You know what the government doesn't need to incentivise? Threesomes and Thorpe Park. Because people already want to do those.

On average, married Brits save £252 a year on tax. Meanwhile, the average cost of a wedding in 2024 was £24,000. For that to pay off you'd have to be married for ninety-five years, with no honeymoon, and hope you make the value of the engagement ring back in Le Creuset crockery on the wedding gift list.

'You're better protected when you're married.' What this means is in the inevitable event that one of you dies, it's much easier for the other one to get the house. Assuming there is a house. I have no qualms with this as a contractual agreement, but do we need to cut a cake about it? If you want to get married for better legal financial protection, by all means go ahead, but those should be your vows. 'Such a beautiful ceremony,' your guests will say. 'I particularly enjoyed when the maid of honour did her reading of the joint tenancy rights.'

Look, I'm not against other people getting married, but when I say I don't want to do it, married people take it personally, as if I'm saying, 'Well, *I* wouldn't get that haircut,' rather than the more accurate, 'Olives just aren't for me.' I even love weddings! I know. How can someone who feels dread about every occasion actually enjoy and look forward to the Mardis Gras of social interaction that is a wedding? A wedding is pretty much all types of party rolled into one. A ceremony, a show, a dinner and a disco. Old friends, complete strangers. It is at the same time formal and informal. You arrive as one person and leave as another. The once polite, suited gentleman 'how do you do'ing his way through the extended family of a schoolfriend he hasn't seen for six years devolves into a crumpled, chanting Neanderthal, at once obsessed with the idea of Eileen coming the fuck on while wondering if the mile-long driveway of a Hertfordshire manor house is too suspicious a location to get a bag delivered. You're a long way from the handheld clothes steamer and lint roller of this morning now, boy. They're fleeting, weddings. They exist for a blip in time and disappear, never to be thought of again by anyone but those who paid for it and the friend they roped in to DJ. If all social interactions were like this, with no overt prospect that we might have to do it again, then life would be easy.

In fact, weddings serve several real-life purposes it's difficult to find anywhere else, especially when it comes to male relationships. Without the 'best man' role, a man is extremely unlikely to tell their best friend that they are just that. But with the formality of a job title, it suddenly becomes acceptable to vocalise those feelings. The best man speech, in fact, for all its mockery, typically ends on a brief burst of sentimentality, somehow permissible for once because you're both dressed like boxing referees. Even as a spectator, outside of the group, getting to see who someone has selected as their best man and how they approach the gig is always an absolute treat. That's why it's disappointing when someone wastes the opportunity to reveal who they rank as their 'number one bestie', and instead reveals who they rank as their brother. And I say that as someone who was his own brother's best man, on what was one of the best days of my life, despite the fact it began with me hung-over and vomiting in my own shoebox.

So it does have merit, marriage, in that it's the only way you're allowed to have a wedding. If marriage was simply about men having a day where it's not awkward to tell their friends how much they like them, I'd be all for it. As it is, I leave my closest friends in limbo, with no confirmation of who would get the nod, but with the ultimate relief that they'll never have to publicly say anything nice about me.

The problem we face at weddings, as a couple of twelve years, is the constant questions of why we haven't done the same thing ourselves. It's very difficult to explain that you don't believe in the thing you've clearly bought a suit and travelled to Cardiff for, not to mention incredibly inappropriate. So we're forced to shrug, as though the thought had never crossed our minds and this is the first we're hearing of the concept. At least with kids you can claim you physically can't have them, so people get uncomfortable and leave you alone. What am I supposed to say about a wedding? 'Oh, we actually can't get married, Daphne doesn't have any fingers.'

I say all this as the child of still-married parents. Much like mobile phones and facial hair, while all my friends were getting their second Christmases, I was made to watch on as love humiliatingly prevailed. My parents did separate for a brief stint when I was fifteen, but by that age all it really meant was an extra holiday, access to a flat in the centre of town and a brand-new iPod. As someone who already had his sights set on a career in the arts, it was a great opportunity for some route-one, surface-level childhood trauma ready to be mined for gold. Sadly, a year later, they got back together, selfishly snatching all that away from me.

If you're in a long-term relationship beyond the age of thirty and you're not married, your relationship is considered less 'serious'. This is because there's nothing more pathetic and infantilising than having to use the word 'girlfriend' as an adult male above a certain age. From thirty up, that word is on a bell curve of acceptability. Thirty to fifty, it's merely embarrassing. Fifty plus, it fluctuates between 'good for you' and abject disgust. Are you bouncing back after a divorce? How sweet. Or did you never marry to begin with? How suspicious. Do you have children with a previous partner, thereby meaning the phrase 'Dad's girlfriend' is currently in use? Well, hey, it's the modern world, and I'm sure they're very supportive. Unless that girlfriend is closer to your children's age than she is to yours? In which case, get a grip, you dirty old sicko. By the time you're in your eighties, you're almost grateful for the respite of being patronised again, as any claim you've got a girlfriend is met with an increased dosage of whatever meds you're on, while your loved ones tell you, 'Sure you do, Grandad. Let me guess, she goes to another retirement home?'

If anything, not being married makes my relationship *more* serious, on account of how easy it would be for either of us to leave. There's no paperwork, no real hassle binding us together. We're here because we want to be. Every time a married person thinks about leaving, they consider all the admin they'll have to get through for the next six months and think, 'Fuck it, I'll just stay here and be unhappy until one of us dies. At least if it's them I can keep the house.' Not me. I could walk out the door at any moment. Not so much as a note. Ten-year relationship concluded at 4 p.m., playing FIFA in my most 'empty cans of Monster' mate's spare room by 5. The fact I don't do this every single day shows you how serious I am about my girlfriend. Despite how unserious that word may be.

It strikes me as illogical that so many relationships suffer at the hands of this socially imposed deadline, when someone loves someone so much they want to spend the rest of their lives with them, so issues a proposal-based ultimatum. But what if that person doesn't want to get married? They'd still like to stay together for ever, but without the paperwork. More often than not, this is a complete no-go, and signifies the end of the relationship. Something that made each party so happy they wanted to do it for ever, now destroyed by a disagreement about admin. Losing out on 'the one' because you'd rather be a wife than be happy. There's a reason every proposal story starts in the same way, with the sentence, 'He had been acting weird all day.' If someone begins an anecdote like that, the ending is either 'and then he proposed' or 'and then he killed everyone'. In any case, it's a life sentence.

Ultimately, what we're all really looking for is security. We want to feel safe, like we can afford to drop the ball once in a while and be a work in progress without being abandoned. That we can open up our houses for the kitten to roam free, without judgement. If we admit that's all we want, then a marriage isn't much more than a locked cat-flap. A big net over the front door. Doing little else but slowing them down when they finally want to call it quits. The average door-sized net on Amazon is £24.50. That's a saving of £23,975.50. It's simple business.

It does seem as though more and more people are starting to figure this out and realise that marriage is one of those things we've evolved past needing, like paper maps, or Richard Madeley. Marriage wasn't originally about love. It was transactional, used to swap daughters for cattle or settle the land disputes of kings. But who has land these days? Or cattle? Or daughters?

The newer generations will look at marriage very differently to those who came before. Like the boomers. Marriage suits the way they were raised. Post-war, in a fit of ongoing Blitz spirit, British boomers like my parents were brought up on the idea of 'stiff upper lip', of mucking in and getting through things no matter how tough they get. This was a virtue. It was character building, and anyone who couldn't graft their way out of, say, a chemical imbalance in their brain was a pansy, or a mad witch who needed a series of electric shocks. The fact I wasn't raised with quite as strict a sentiment suggests my parents don't necessarily agree with it any more, but hearing that sort of stuff at such a formative age seeps in. The boomers are resilient. They don't give up. Try having a conversation with one! But they're also stubborn. *They don't give up.* Do you know how insane that is, to not give up, even when it's so obvious you should? But if you've been told your whole life that quitters are society's greatest scourge, then of course you stick it out.

Lots of toxic influencers of today try to push the same angle, that quitters never win and winners never quit. That may be true, but it only takes one episode of *Britain's Got Talent*'s early rounds to see that quite a lot of losers never quit either. There are plenty of stalkers who never quit. Is that a virtue? This is the paradox of good old-fashioned British resilience. The image we have of ourselves mucking in and fighting until the last breath like heroes, while the rest of the world looks at us as a group of pale, toothless bigots lovelessly clutching on to the Elgin Marbles like a spoilt toddler who never learned to share. The Commonwealth looms sadly in the background like a WhatsApp group for a stag do we went on several years ago, full of people who didn't want to be in it in the first place, and only used now to occasionally ask if anyone wants to do some sport.

This 'resilience' the boomers grew up on is carried with them for ever. They get through recessions by putting their shoulders back and exercising portion control. They get through pandemics by standing on their driveways and banging their pots with wooden spoons. They get through undiagnosed gluten intolerance by accepting diarrhoea as part of their daily lives. And most importantly, they get through marriage by staring over their glasses at the TV while single-finger prodding their iPads in silence, then plastering on a smile when they bump into the neighbours. 'Keep Calm and Carry On' doesn't feel like such a ridiculous policy when your marriage actually is in the trenches. Sure, some of them do get divorced, but they're so obsessed with definites and extremes they spend the rest of their lives referring to it as a 'failed marriage'. Failed? You completed it! Rejoice. You've defeated the final boss, now go out and start the sequel. That's how much boomers love marriage: they often have three of them.

Younger generations aren't like this. They don't refuse to give up when faced with hardship. Some criticise them for giving up at even the slightest hint that hardship may be down the line. Gen Z in particular are quitting the workforce at a rate never before seen in history. Perhaps from a lack of hardiness, or maybe because they've seen through a game rigged against them, that the promises of yesteryear no longer apply, that for them it's not a corporate ladder but a Gladiator's travelator constantly disappearing beneath their feet. Or perhaps it's because of the way they were raised. Contrary to the boomers Daniel Bedingfielding their way 'thru this', Gen Z were brought up on the idea of 'know your worth', 'never settle for anything less than you deserve', and 'dump his ass'. They grew up with iPads, phones and social media, which, whatever other debatable toxic consequences aside, undoubtedly aided the corrosion of their patience and attention spans. How, then, are Gen Z going to enter into a *contract*, with a partner they actually deem *good enough . . . until death*?

Heterosexual marriage rates have declined with every generation, even since before the baby boomers. It is a dying medium you'd be foolish to invest in, like minidiscs or non-fiction comedy books. Millennials already get married less than boomers, Gen Z even less than millennials, and the generation below Gen Z (Gen Alpha) have a marriage rate of 0 per cent. If that isn't conclusive proof, I don't know what is.

And sure, maybe I underestimate the innate human desire for pageantry. Some would argue the attention-seeking nature of an influencer generation lends itself perfectly to, if not marriage, weddings, which, with all their look-at-me grandiosity are effectively mini coronations but no one's allowed to say your fingers look fat. But why would you need to bother spending thousands of pounds to make one day all about you when platforms exist in the palm of your hand that can make every day about you? And *earn* you money. More to the point, why traverse the murky dating pool in search of 'understanding' when a few thumbs up emojis can validate the same gap in your soul? Why walk the tightrope of being fancied face-to-face, at the mercy of how you are perceived, when an OnlyFans, on which you control the edit, can do the trick much more reliably, like a sort of self-produced *Truman Show*? The best-case scenario if you get married is the right of attorney to let your partner switch off your life support machine so they can keep your maisonette. Well, as I'm sure Gen Z would say, 'What maisonette?' Surely the safer option is, as usual, to do nothing. To stay online, to control the narrative. A place, for all its faults, that ultimately gives us the answer we're all looking for: somewhere you actually can be all of yourself at once, or none of yourself at all. And you'll never have to spend a Friday night at Flight Club making chit-chat with the Townsends.

Or perhaps you get lucky, and you find someone early. Someone who makes you realise that the reason you find certain social situations so exhausting is because you're faking them, you're 'switching it on', but you never feel tired around her because there's no performance, everything's real. Someone who doesn't drain your battery, but charges it. Someone who actually makes you want to push through your self-doubt and anxiety, because your presence at her side makes her happy and hers at yours makes you proud. Someone with whom you did get a kitten and did let it roam around the entire house immediately and it did shit on your sofa and it didn't matter at all. Someone who makes you question if you're truly against marriage as a concept, or if you're against it as an activity. If your precious principles hold firm in the face of any pushback, or if this is another opportunity to say, 'Oh, you don't want to go? Me neither! Let's stay in and get a takeaway, every night, for ever.' Someone you'd propose to in a heartbeat if it was at all important to her, because she's one of the very few people who has ever made you feel like you. Who makes you realise you don't need to be understood by everyone, but just one person. Who proves that a logical dismantling of marriage holds no weight in the battle against emotion, and to trade all your cattle and sign a lifelong statistically untenable contract with her would be an honour. But who doesn't need all that, because love is not a series of milestones or checkpoints. Love is not a net over your porch. Love is the freedom to leave at any moment. Love is . . . and here's one for all the new parents . . . Love is an open door.

But I Am le Tired

'Call me Penguin,' I said to my peer group of ten-year-olds, who were focused more on chasing the sponge ankle-roll death-trap we called a 'football' around the playground than listening to my commands. 'Huh?' came back one disinterested voice. 'Penguin. That's what I want you to call me from now on.' And thus began a lifelong trend of trying to start my own nickname. This one caught on for about four hours, as one friend James noted I did look a bit like a penguin in my winter coat with the slightly too-long arms, thus it checked out as something they might've come up with to mock me on their own. Nicknames in Britain have to come from a place of bullying, or they're unsatisfying. Typically they follow the actual joke formula of 'we call him X because Y', such as 'we call him bungalow because there's nothing going on upstairs', or 'we call him Turpin, because he's a dick'. As a ten-year-old, however, nicknames are more basic. A friend and I once waited outside the school toilets to uncover which mystery pupil had been noisily partaking in the indignity of an at-school bowel movement. Hearing our fake exit, Will Carpenter emerged from the cubicle assuming the coast was clear, only to be referred to as Will Poopenter from then on.

With no sense of organic bullying, there's no sense of fun, so it's no surprise that 'Penguin' didn't fully stick. But if my friends had any clue where I'd got the idea from, they'd have such bully fodder I'd still be known as Penguin to this day.

I'm part of a generation that falls under the umbrella of 'digital natives'. People who grew up surrounded by technology and have always understood it as part of their everyday lives. Bored in maths one day, age thirteen, I eavesdropped on a conversation between two of my classmates, Annie and Craig, discussing a girl Craig had been chatting to online. He was talking about how much he liked her and how much it seemed she liked him. Jealous and parroting a criticism I'd heard a thousand times, I interrupted to say, 'Have you ever actually spoken in real life?' Both of them turned around, and at the same time, with complete conviction, said to me: 'This *is* real life.' It remains the most profound thing I've ever heard.

But the digital world we're natives of wasn't always like it is now. In my day there were no iPad kids, phones couldn't record videos, and social media was still just a break-up revenge fantasy in the subconscious of Harvard's biggest incel. The most important bit of technology we had was a single, enormous desktop computer in the family 'study', equipped with Encarta 96 (an offline Wikipedia or digital textbook, on an actual disc, featuring interactive videos and games which would trick you into learning about Napoleon when you thought you were having fun), Fury3 (a flight-simulation space-war game controlled with a joystick, which required some pretty hefty squinting to make out what you were supposedly shooting at) and Microsoft Paint (a design program on which you'd write your own name over and over again, usually with a spray can, until you discovered Word-Art and wrote it there instead).

The internet, still in its relative infancy, wasn't the vast metropolis we know now, with its financial empires, millionaire influencers and easily accessible exposed flesh. It was a lawless wasteland waiting to be built on. These days, the internet is like Dubai, whereas thirty-odd years ago, the internet was like Dubai thirty-odd years ago. Back then, we weren't warned of things like digital footprints. We weren't scared we might one day get called out for an eleven-year-old tweet. We were simply scared of getting catfished in a chat room by a sex pest pretending to be 11 years old. There wasn't an algorithm that knew what we wanted to see before we did; there was an impossibly slow loading process that would show us what we wanted to see long after we didn't any more.

These days, the internet can be your bank, teacher, doctor and therapist. It can predict what you might say, create live 3D renderings of your own face as a different gender, write movie scripts, pay for your parking, order drinks to your table, do everything short of tying your shoelace. When I was a kid, it could make some text look like it was on fire. You couldn't 'stream' TV, or even pornography, on the internet, but you could ask a nice butler called Jeeves to find you a photo of Pamela Anderson, so long as you were willing to have a sit-down chat with your parents about it two days later, having made the mistake of printing it. You couldn't listen to music on Spotify, but you could illegally download a song over three days, putting the computer largely out of action for the duration, with no way of knowing it would actually be the correct one. You couldn't carefully curate an online profile of your life to entice brands to give you money, but you could learn an entirely new language of code, made up mostly of symbols, in order to create your own unique web page that said exactly the same thing as everyone else's: 'Welcome to my website!!!!!1'

Now look, I liked 'playing out' as much as the next kid. I
had a bike and I was good at 'kerby', and one summer a
bunch of haystacks got put into the field at the end of my
road, so every night after school, the entire year group hung
out there until it got dark, shouting 'Jackass!' as we'd jump
from the top of a haystack, or flirtatiously giving girls our
McKenzie hoodies to wear while they sat at the bottom.
Every day at school, kids would widen their eyes and say in
frenzied whispers, 'Haystacks tonight?' like a horse couple
making dinner plans. It was the greatest two weeks of my
life.

But for an introverted little dweeb like me, the internet, in
all its shiny novelty, was the real place to be. The internet was
exciting. Free from the scrutiny of your classmates, it was a
chance to reinvent yourself. But not in the way people think
university is a chance to reinvent yourself, where people can
still actually *see* you. The internet was somewhere you could
be anyone you claimed to be, and no one could prove you
weren't. I chose to be me. What an idiot.

Well, not exactly me. Little cartoon versions of me, swanning around a cartoon version of a hotel. Specifically, Habbo
Hotel. For those of you over or under a certain age, and over
or under a certain social ability, Habbo Hotel was a sort of
interactive virtual world full of real strangers. You were all
mini avatars, like cheaper Sims, communicating via speech
bubbles above your character's head. The Wikipedia for
Habbo Hotel claims it's an online game, though I don't know
what the objective is, except for not getting nonced. The
Encarta 96 entry for Habbo Hotel does not exist.

Habbo Hotel wasn't even the only one of its kind: there
was also Club Penguin, an identical format set in the tundra,
in which everyone is their own penguin. The strapline of the

game was 'waddle around and meet new friends', something I had been taking incredibly literally in real life thanks to my big coat. Remarkably, Club Penguin was not where I got the idea for my nickname. I never ventured so far as the virtual Arctic, choosing instead to stay in my virtual hotel, a microcosm for my entire life. I was, for my sins, incredibly loyal to Habbo, though such loyalty was not rewarded with points in the way it would be at a Hilton.

That's not to say there weren't perks at the Hab. Of course there were. The internet hadn't become the full penny-wringing mega-enterprise it is today, but it still cashed in on loneliness like every other platform. In Habbo Hotel, you had your own individual room, like a normal hotel, and for that room you could purchase better furniture, like a normal hotel (that you own). One day after school, swanning around my lodgings, mostly milling about in my own room as I plucked up the courage to head to the bar, I noticed a brand-new sofa against a previously bare wall. What was this? Had I unlocked it by spending so much time on the platform? Had I been upgraded for being so charming downstairs? Before I could delude myself further, the tiny cartoon version of my friend Nathan appeared in my room, ignoring the 'do not disturb' sign, to ask if I liked my new 'furni'.

The next morning at school he reliably informed me he'd found this magical card covered in embossed numbers in his mum's purse, and if you typed the numbers into your computer, it opened up a whole new world of possibility.

That night, Nathan and I raced around the communal areas of Habbo Hotel trying to entice everyone we could with the promise of free home furnishings. We were like Oprah Winfrey, yelling, 'You get a chair, you get a chair!' from our speech bubbles to the hundreds of tiny digital spongers putting their hands out. In my head, those other avatars always belonged to adults, letting off steam after a hard day's work on the courtroom floor or the operating table. In reality, they were probably bozos like us, who happened to have slightly less trusting mothers. Either way, for one night only, age nine, on our parents' desktop computers, we lived the lives of Russian billionaires, quaffing pixelated Cristal with our legions of purchased friends, until a few days later when Nathan's mum received her credit card bill in the post and went understandably mental. It's one thing being stung by hidden extra charges in a real hotel, but paying to furnish a fake cartoon hotel on behalf of two nine-year-olds takes the absolute piss, and we were promptly banned from the establishment.

So, on to the next one, an in-browser RPG game called Alien Adoption Agency (AlienAA). In this one, you created an alien that could fight other aliens, earning you 'angel' or 'devil' points. To ensure you won said fights you could train your alien in the gym or buy weapons with 'alien bucks' you'd get by sending your alien to 'work', or trading 'bytes' on the 'stock market'. I guess the message of the game was that capitalism isn't just an Earth thing? To clarify, none of this actually visually happened. There was an image of your alien at the top of the page (a little green fellow who looked exactly like what popped into your brain when you read the word 'alien'), but other than that, you were informed of its progress in text form, usually in real time. If event television has been ruined by streaming platforms releasing all episodes at once, then gaming has surely been obliterated by continual gameplay. On AlienAA, if you sent your alien off to work, you'd have to come back tomorrow to see how much money they had made. The suspense was agonising.

Of course, this sort of game always came with a forum, where its users gathered to chat tactics, call each other 'noob' and, in my case, outright ask for money. Some call it begging, I call it venture capital. Plus, I was ten years old, and therefore allowed to be as cheeky as I liked. Admittedly it's probably not quite what Charles Dickens imagined when he wrote *Oliver Twist* ('Please, sir, can I have some more alien bucks?'), but all the classics have their modern adaptations, and at least I wasn't doing a rap version of *Romeo and Juliet*. I went with a simple post explaining how I was new to the game and really wanted to buy a new outfit for my alien, but hadn't earned any money yet, and I'm just an innocent little boy trying to make it in this harsh world, mister. The next day I got home from school to discover 36,500 game dollars deposited into my alien account. I couldn't believe it, a year's alien salary in a single donation! It was like the sofa all over again. Had Nathan found another loophole, or another Amex? I instant messaged him to find out, but he had no idea of the source either and was incredibly jealous. I logged back into the forum and returned to my post, under which there was one reply, which simply read: 'Since you asked so nicely.' I scanned across the page and read the username . . . Penguin.

Username selection was undeniably an art form, and not one I had yet mastered. Typically I would misinterpret the sign-up form and register with my actual full name, so on a forum full of d0nkeybongs, mister_wassups and bigdawg123s, there'd be a rogue *Rhys Jones*, which must've given the impression of a stern grown-up looking over his glasses at the kids to make sure they're behaving, when in fact, it was the exact opposite. For those of you who haven't studied my Wikipedia entry, Jones is my real surname, changed out of necessity a few years into my comedy career due to the existence of another

Rhys Jones in an acting union that, much like a forum, only allows one member per name. I could've taken the online route and gone for a stage name of Rhys_Jones69, or even forced comedy clubs to introduce me as 'Penguin', but instead, my agent suggested I opt for the closest actual name to my real one, Rhys James. The fact there is now a Champions League-winning footballer with practically the same name while the 'actor' Rhys Jones is nowhere to be seen is proof that nothing ever goes my way. Then again, the fact Chelsea's Reece James is almost constantly injured is all the proof I need that praying actually works. We go again.

Before you could even sign up to anything with a user-name, you had to have an email address. This was the original username, and far more significant. For parents, it was all: first name dot surname at BTinternet dot com. Nothing to think about. My grandparents even had a shared couple's email address (girl, if he wanted to, he would!) at something called 'Tiscali'. But for the Hotmail generation, things weren't so simple. An email address wasn't just an email address; it was an act of expression, an attempt to boil down our most distinctive personality traits or physical tells into a pithy moniker, possibly featuring an underscore or the year of our birth. It was an acceptable attempt to start your own nickname.

My first email address, little__legend@hotmail.com, had pretty simple origins. I was little, I felt I was a legend, and I wasn't the first to do so, hence the double underscore. Other highlights from my school included 'hamsterkiller_hair', from my spiky-barneted friend Tim; 'BlackYaris1', from a girl called Jess, who, at twelve, was clearly extremely into 1-litre Toyota hatchbacks; and one of the all-time classics from my old pal Fred – 'stacys_dad'. Your email address was a part of your identity. Unlike the forum username, it wasn't just strangers on the internet who would see this; your entire friendship group would eventually come across it, and if you didn't change it in time, you'd find yourself having to reluctantly say it out loud to an estate agent round the corner from your university.

There were several other efforts along the way, from 'littlepunk91' and 'RJlinkinpark', to 'psychojones11' – another failed attempt to ward off potential bullies, who, it turns out, seldom ask for your email address before stealing your wallet. For millennials, the 'first email address' chat has become a staple third-pint indulgence down memory lane that ends up being a great exposé into what sort of child you were, your popularity level and your now embarrassing interests of yore. More telling than any of the addresses for me in particular was the fact I had four of them. Whenever this conversation comes up, people ask me why a child would need four email addresses. Like seeing an adult with two phones, your mind instantly goes to one of three options: drug dealer, celebrity, horny freak. What did people think of me as a kid with four emails? AOL fraudster? GeoCities magnate? Horny freak? I certainly wouldn't want to have to deny any of them under oath.

But before email, there was the landline telephone. There was no opportunity for showmanship in the phone number, but there was certainly some playground kudos in being able to memorise them. From your own, to your friends', to the financial institutions that advertised on television (Chelsea Building Society, 0800 341341, and I did not need to google that), reciting phone numbers was an art form. So, unsurprisingly, prior to the digital playground that was the early internet, I bashed away at the buttons on my parents' landline every night after school, frantically making calls like an eighties banker on the trading floor.

Primarily, I ran up enormous bills phoning into competitions on Nickelodeon forty times a day, never getting through but being charged for each attempt. In hindsight, the kids' TV phone-in contest is possibly the greatest financial con in history. Forget Bernie Madoff, Lehman Brothers or even Charles Ponzi himself. The greatest economic scam artist in history is 'James Llewlyn-Smellen' urging a seven-year-old me to get on the phone to answer a question with such an insanely obvious answer it would literally be an insult to my own intelligence not to win myself a PlayStation. Of course I'm going to do that! I'm a child. It doesn't matter if you tell me calls cost £1.50 per minute, I have no concept of money. Every time I've ever actually wanted anything it's either been provided by a friend's oblivious mum or a stranger on an alien forum.

It didn't even have to be a competition. I would phone in to Nickelodeon to try and get on in the between-programme segments, where a goofy adult man dressed like Tyler the Creator would natter with a child about what they did at school, before asking if they liked *Hey Arnold!* in order to throw to the next programme. It was effectively Babestation, but instead of giving men the chance to chat with a *Nuts* magazine pin-up who would never give them the time of day in person, it was for children to cosplay conversations with grown-up cousin figures, who were forced to be nice to them for fear of losing their job. Once again, the internet has replaced both of these concepts: chatting with 'babes' is now done via cam-girl pop-ups or OnlyFans, and conversations with slightly older boys is done via the chat sidebar on gamers' Twitch streams. Back then, you had to say everything you wanted to say to these people *out loud*, via *wired* phones in your *parents'* hallway. I was addicted to the stuff, and I'm convinced I'm the reason they now say, 'Always ask the bill payer's permission.'

Elsewhere, I made significantly cheaper but equally annoying local calls to my friend Tom's home phone. Once you learn a phone number as a child, there's really no choice but to dial it every ten seconds until you're old enough to drink alcohol. One afternoon, after endless cold calls, Tom's mum eventually answered the phone with an immediate and very stern: 'Rhys, please stop calling here.' Being the generational wit I am, I responded equally quickly in a thick xenophobic accent: 'I am not Rhys, I am French.'

Checkmate. Or should I say, check*ami*. You've been bested, Mrs Tom's Mum. We both know there couldn't possibly be a Frenchman called Rhys, so what's your move now, eh? I am simply making this pricey international call from Paris to ask if your son is home, and you choose to treat me with such rudeness? Well, I shan't be insulted in this way on my own telephone. I bid you adieu. If you'd like to speak about this further, you can reach me at petitlegende_@'otmail.com.

So back online, and on to my next sordid little role-play forum secret. This one, a multiplayer competition called Project Rockstar. You're manager to a band, setting them to practise, write and release 'music', and eventually tour, while you choose marketing spend, select venues and design album covers. Like AlienAA, the game updated overnight and you'd rush back online to see if you had the coveted number-one single, against thousands of other losers doing the exact same thing. Once again, the songs themselves didn't exist, it was all just text on an orange screen. Effectively, it was Football Manager but for music, if every footballer and team was fictional and made up by someone else playing the game. And unlike Football Manager, where you might brag to your real-life friends about taking Swindon from League Two to the top half of the Premier League, I kept my progress from dingy pubs to Wembley Stadium with 'The Salt and Vinegars' very much to myself.

In Project Rockstar, which is possibly the most embarrassing name to say you're rushing home to check the progress of, it was less about the gameplay, and more about the community. It too had a forum, but unlike any other game I'd played, the forum was the main part of the experience. In fact, getting fictional radio-play became background pretty quickly to a close-knit global community, there to discuss all sorts of things from TV shows to personal gripes, funny family stories all the way to collectively talking people down from suicide. Some of the more creative members of the gang even wrote and recorded actual songs about the community to post on the forum, which, I remind you, was the forum of a game all about *pretending* to write *fake* songs. Mind-boggling.

The community was so strong, they would do yearly meet-ups in London parks and pubs, returning online the next day to post photos, so I could play my own game attempting to match the username to the real-life goth. I never attended any of the meet-ups, on account of being slightly too cool, and way too thirteen for it not to be the literal worst nightmare of a mum convinced everyone on the internet was there solely to kidnap Rhys Jones. But I was a big player on those forums. A main character due to nothing more than the quantity of my posting. In fact, many of that community have since come to watch me on tour, in what my mother likely still thinks are failed attempts to bundle me into a van.

I don't know why it feels so embarrassing to reveal all this, like I'm admitting to a secret identity. It's no lamer to me than being active on TikTok or Instagram, which isn't to say it's not lame, but that those things are also completely pathetic endeavours. On the Project Rockstar forums, there was something called 'star points', which were rewards for posting something useful or hilarious. Is that so different to harvesting likes? After a certain amount of star points, little star graphics appeared under your username, to let everyone know you were better than them. Is that so different to the blue tick? And why was I training myself to seek this kind of validation from such a young age? The difference with star points is that they couldn't be given out by just anyone. You had to be an admin to have that kind of power, and once I grew out of my pursuit of receiving star points, I became absolutely hell-bent in my quest to be able to bestow them. It was no longer enough to be one of the forum's most vocal players. I had to be in charge.

There were a few ways to become an admin, beyond being an employed developer of the game. The most common was to be one of the forum's eldest users, which usually meant you were around forty-five, giving you a base of authority, and making it unlikely you'd abuse such power. This one wasn't an option for me, obviously. Another was to be constantly online and attending regular meet-ups. Halfway there. Some became admin simply from receiving so many star points that the number of stars under their name earned them a promotion, which is also how they do it at McDonald's. The quickest way to get those star points was to be funny, and this had been my plan for a while. But despite consistently earning myself an impressive haul of stars for my jokes, I still wasn't getting the nod from the powers that be. A feeling I would go on to have five more times with the Edinburgh Comedy Awards. In reality, being funny wasn't enough, and I was overlooked due to a combination of my youth and my refusal to engage in the in-person schmoozing and social climbing all the other losers were so desperate to do. But enough about those comedy awards.

Gradually, in Project Rockstar, another route to power emerged. In the game's attempts to expand its audience, the developers had begun a process of translating it into different languages. As such a tight community, they preferred when this was done by one of the characters on the forum, partly because they would understand the ins and outs of the game better than a regular translator, but mainly because they were suckers who would do it for free. I watched as Greek, Italian and German forum users (with far fewer star points than me, for crying out loud) got bumped up to admin status, based on the sole criteria that they could offer a service. Thus, having failed to get my flowers on pure vibes, I saw an opportunity. After all, I am not Rhys. I am *French*.

Writing to Chris, the creator of the game, I explained that I spoke fluent French, and could easily translate the entire game for him. I was clever enough to not even mention the word admin, so as to convince him I had no hidden agenda, merely a love of gendered nouns and increased potential user bases. Chris was receptive to the idea, and sent me three trial pages of game text to translate for him, in order to prove myself. Needless to say, despite being an incredibly precocious nightmare who clearly had lots of time on my hands, I could not speak French. Sure, I could make a pretty convincing argument that I *was* French over the phone, but this was online, where my accent alone wouldn't carry, and I'd have to know the actual words. Unfortunately for me, none of the text I had been sent involved libraries, swimming pools or breakfast, so I was completely out of my depth. But this changed nothing. I knew I couldn't speak French when I suggested this whole thing, but I also knew about a secret website called freetranslation.com, on which you could paste in any text and it would instantly translate it all for you, completely free of charge. What a fool Chris was, for not knowing about this website, but instead employing actual humans to translate his game, also for free. Mug. I copied Chris's pages into the text box, selected 'English to French' and clicked go. Ten seconds later, my homework was done.

Obviously I'm not stupid. I didn't send it back instantly, that would've given the game away. I waited a full day before returning the text, now all nice and sexy-sounding, to add to the sense of realism. Not so fast he'd know it was automated, but not so slow he'd think I was a slacker. The perfect patsy. *Bellissimo!*

Chris, however, was more prompt. He responded ten minutes later to inform me my translation was insane, entirely literal, and clearly the work of a moron who has copied and pasted it into a free translation website. My services would not be required, in part because they didn't exist.

The admin dream was dead. For the second time in three years I had claimed to be French, once in an attempt to evade criticism, another in a bid to gain status. Both had failed miserably. Then again, a self-proclaimed 'little legend' attempting to seize power via the French language? Perhaps those days on Encarta 96 weren't wasted.

Astonishingly, this isn't even the final time I tried to peddle my Gallic credentials, repeating the act only a few years ago in Manchester. I truly am the boy who cried *escargot*. One evening, post-show, walking back to my hotel (real, not Habbo), I saw a hooded young gentleman approaching people ahead of me, asking them for 'the time'. I knew this question was designed to make you take out your phone, which he'd then yank out of your hand and sprint off with. Ahead of me, the boy approached a Japanese couple, who I had definitely heard speaking English, but who suddenly pretended they couldn't understand him. To be honest, with his thick Manchester accent even I was struggling, so maybe they weren't lying. As they responded to him exclusively in Japanese, the would-be mugger lost patience and gave up, moving on to his next target – me.

'Oi lad, you got the time?' It was ten past ten, but knowing that once I revealed I was English there was no going back, I said simply: 'Par-*don*?'

My accent was thick. Almost cartoonish. It may help to imagine it coming from a set of lips under the thinnest, curliest moustache, beneath the reddest beret you've ever seen. That's certainly what I was imagining as I got into the role. '*Pardon garçon? Je ne comprends pas.*'

Bang. How's that for fluent French, Chris, you gatekeeping role-play game-developing nerd! 'Pardon, sir. I do not understand!' Stick that in your cigarette and flick it pretentiously.

'You French?' said the boy.

'Eeeh,' I said, like Arsène Wenger pretending not to have seen a controversial penalty decision.

'Errr . . . *Français*?' he said, in his Manchester accent. Brief panic from me as I considered the fact he may speak better French than I do, as I was already close to my limit.

'*Oui, oui! Français!*' I said enthusiastically, all while still rudely walking at a considerable pace to try and both lose him and stay in character.

'Which part . . . er . . . *où, le* . . . area *de . . . Français* are you from? *Habite? HABITE!!*'

If nothing else, my fake Frenchness had at least distracted him, piquing an interest in something other than stealing my phone. Perhaps education does work? But where in France am I from, he wanted to know? I rattled off the cities in my head. Can't be Paris, too obvious, even if statistically quite likely. Not Nice, that feels too much like a holiday destination to be somewhere anyone actually lives. He doesn't look like a film buff, but keen to avoid Cannes, for fear he pivots the conversation onto Fellini. Briefly toyed with saying Juan-les-Pins, a tiny village I had visited on holiday as a kid, but thought it may be showing off *too much* knowledge, and possibly wealth. And so, with time running out, I offered the one remaining French option in my brain at the time.

'Toulouse,' I said with a whimper.

'Toulouse?' he queried back, his face now scrunched.

'Toulouse,' I said again. If I'd thrown in a 'to me' we could have invented the French Chuckle Brothers. '*Les Frères Chuckelle*'.

'Toulouse . . .' he considered, stopping his stride. 'I'll have to look it up.'

By this point I was about ten paces away from him as he stood frozen in contemplation. A few more steps and he called out to me.

'Oh . . . erm . . . *au revoir*! *Bon* . . err . . . *Bon nuit*! *Bon nuit!!*'

I waved back, satisfied that I had successfully evaded a mugging without even having to tell him I play football with my brother and go to the cinema with my dad, and delighted that after all these years of training on the phone and online, pretending to be French had finally paid off in real life. Actual *'real life'*.

The internet was a curious prospect when I was a kid. It had been around for a while, but only as some scrolling green matrix text for Bill Gates to look at. When my generation got to it, it was starting to branch out into something interesting. I've seen people my age criticise what a Wild West it was, how its newness meant our parents were not yet aware of the damage it could do to our growing minds, and the negative impacts of letting us roam free on it, unmonitored. I find it hard to believe a generation obsessed with telling us germs build immunity and breaking our arms builds character would've done anything to protect us even if they had known. Young parents today literally went through the process of destroying their own attention spans on social media, and still respond to a crying toddler by handing them an iPad. We all admit defeat before kick-off.

Regardless, we didn't really need protection from the internet back then. There was no unknowable algorithm to fear, or ban. 'Social media' was just something called MSN Messenger and AI was an MSN chatbot called Smarter-Child. You didn't covet approval in a faceless like-count on a highly edited photo of your own body like you do now. MSN was about conversation. Specifically, with people you were often too shy to speak to in real life. It was texting, before we decided we're all OK with children having phones, and before texting became Snapchat, and Snapchat became Flimple or whatever the fuck it is now. If you wanted to get your crush's attention on MSN, you didn't 'like' their story, or post a picture of yourself next to another girl. You simply signed in and out over and over again, so your name appeared in their sidebar multiple times. MSN wasn't so much about your image, or how you appeared. Sure, you had a screen name, but that was to be filled with some of the most emo lyrics you've ever heard in alternating caps and lower case, with a few ~ symbols and heart emoticons either side for good measure. My screen name, of course, was Rhys William Jones. Tom's was []D[][]\/[][]D. If someone found our chat logs they'd assume they were of a solicitor conversing with his client. It was a simpler time.

Outside of communication, the internet was a creative hub. People often talk about YouTube in its infancy being a place for grainy public expression, for ideas to be brought to life and for genuine, real, earned virality to flourish – before it became a system to be gamed for huge profits. But these were the days even before YouTube. When websites like eBaum's World and Albino Blacksheep would collect mad sketches and dumb images from around the globe, solely to make you laugh. Ideas from the bizarre, like a pixelated dancing banana informing us it's 'peanut butter jelly time', or a cartoon explanation of exactly how World War III was going to start, to *America's Funniest Home Videos*-style mini clips of a teenager recreating a *Star Wars* light-sabre fight scene on his own, or a middle-aged man enthusiastically singing along to 'Numa Numa' in his bedroom. These wouldn't scratch the surface today. In some ways that's good, we've grown more sophisticated with our memes, but I still feel somewhat remorseful about the fact a panda could sneeze on its own baby tomorrow and no one would even sharply exhale out of their nose.

The internet was all about creativity. If I wasn't managing

a fictional rock band, I was creating another email nickname, or adopting an extraterrestrial. And when I wasn't doing any of that, I was spending an inordinate amount of time writing and rewriting short stories for something called an 'eFed'. The eFed was yet another forum, this time not populated with strangers, but boys from my school. It wasn't to bitch or even chat, but a creative writing exercise, on which you built your own identity as a wrestler, got drawn against other wrestlers, then wrote up the 'story' of your wrestling match as creatively as possible, often including 'cool' graphics like barbed-wire paragraph dividers, or scene headings that glowed. You would then be judged by the other 'wrestlers' on categories such as realism, writing style, visual flair and so on. We were effectively escaping the stress of school by going home to voluntarily sit our own made-up English exams. My wrestler was undefeated. I called him 'The Penguin'. It was that or 'Rhys Jones'.

Eventually though, the creative innocence of all of this died out, with the dominance of social media. MySpace allowed for some minimal creativity in both your username and your 'Top 8' friend selection, which proved whether or not you were seriously concerned with social cachet, or an actual laugh ('Rhys has got Lily Allen and Mr Wilson in his top 8, lmao!' etc.). I found brief local infamy via MySpace for my catchy and extremely clever pseudonym, 'Rhys Actually' (like Love Actually, but Rhys), which people would call me in the street, mockingly. A lesson in never deviating from what you know best: using your full given name for everything.

Of course, once Facebook turned up, things became more about showing yourself to have a vibrant nightlife and a large university friendship group, uploading albums from every night out to show that you are capable of both getting very drunk and holding your phone at full arm's length from your head. This eventually moved on to the more public and curated lifestyle porn of Instagram, on which the currency became envy, as people pined for a life or body they had been shown but didn't really exist, eventually evolving into 'realism porn', on which people would show their *real* bodies alongside their edited pictures under the guise of 'mental health', but really as a way to have their cake and not eat it too.

Online creativity may still have its place on TikTok and YouTube, but it's all done with the quiet expectation that, if not now, someday, it might make you a million pounds. Even so, the rise of the 'algorithm', which curates a perfect playlist of content based on our own individual viewing habits on something called the 'for you' page, has destroyed any need for a creator to actually attract 'followers'. Videos you post on TikTok and YouTube are no longer pushed out to the people who actually subscribe to your work, instead favouring strangers who have interacted with something similar. This has short-term appeal, because it's easier to go viral, but the prospect of building a community of like-minded people gradually disappears in the rear-view mirror. And even as a viewer, I've had so many conversations with friends that suggest their own 'for you' page is completely different to mine. Things that have become mainstay references to them, I've never heard of, and vice versa. The relentless pursuit of these platforms to keep the individual looking at them at all costs has massively dulled the possibility of real-life connection over a shared viewing experience. We're forced to report back to each other on our findings from our own corners of the algorithm like archaeologists on opposite sides of the world.

I long for the days of an internet that couldn't make me any money. Not real money, anyway. But one that could give me an outlet and a community. I miss people making things because they had an idea, rather than an idea of how to get rich. I miss when the internet felt like a place you could go, rather than a gas that engulfs us, an oxygen we need to live. I miss when I could decide I wanted to be called 'Penguin' without having to consider Search Engine Optimisation. Mostly, I miss when the internet was something you could escape to, rather than something people constantly talk about trying to spend less time on.

Being a 'digital native' is far more than growing up around technology. Eventually, it becomes the yearning for aspects of technology that no longer exist. Project Rockstar and EBaum's World feel like actual places to me. Places I can no longer visit, because they've been knocked down and paved over. The day word got round that they'd removed the hay-stacks from the field, kids mourned them like they'd lost a part of themselves. Had we got to experience them for a further week before they were taken away, we might've been emboldened enough to march, like Northerners in a film where they've knocked down the community centre.

The internet as I knew it didn't have its closing down day. It happened gradually, without us realising, as it morphed into something bigger and more omniscient. But what a glorious thing it used to be, and how important it was, as a nervous kid, to have this resource I could call upon to express myself, when I may have been too scared to in person. Another world I could go to when I couldn't handle the pressures of the real one.

I never deleted any of my accounts on those old platforms. Project Rockstar no longer exists, but AlienAA and

Habbo Hotel are still readily available. For all I know, my alien still pops off to work every day, and my Habbo avatar still wanders around that lobby, not saying much, just taking up space. I like to think I instilled enough of my own personality into that guy that he's continuing on in my image. If so, he's probably hiding in his room right now, sitting on his complimentary sofa, scrolling on his laptop, and trying to convince someone, somewhere, that he is, indeed, French.

No Kidding

You never know you're truly ready to become an uncle, it sort of just happens. One day you're a regular guy, popping out for coffees in East London, writing jokes about your own butt, living selfishly. The next, your life is turned upside down. All change. Nothing can prepare you for that phone call when your brother tells you your sister-in-law is pregnant, you just hope your honest reaction is positive. 'Wow,' I thought, 'they seem happy, but am I prepared for this? I'm so young. And I wasn't even consulted!'

I knew instantly that life would never be the same again, that some of my weekends were now going to be spent in the playground bit of the park rather than the artisan food market bit of the park. Is this the end of my life, or the beginning of a new one? I said my congratulations and went off to put a cold flannel on my neck to calm down.

It's been long established in our relationship that we don't want kids of our own. Or anyone else's, for that matter – there's nothing worse than a stranger's kids. It was something we discussed alarmingly quickly as a pair of naive idiots in our early twenties who weren't even an exclusive couple yet, and despite being patronised by everyone older than us that this would change, we have so far stuck to it into our thirties.

Expressing your lack of desire for children as a man yields

wildly different results to doing the same thing as a woman. 'Well, of course,' seems to be the consensus towards men. 'You've got your career to focus on, and that window to stare out of while clinking ice around that whisky glass, and thinking about the war . . . How could you possibly be expected to raise a child?' But for women there's a palpable disgust. 'What are you going to do with your time if not breastfeed? What are you going to keep in your bag if not wet wipes?'

Even when we were younger, people would try to convince us we were wrong. 'Oh, you will,' they'd say to Daphne. 'No one wants kids at your age, but once your friends have them you'll start to feel broody.' I appreciate people are playing the averages, but if they're going by what most people do, surely they should laugh out loud when someone says, ''Til death do us part,' and give it the big, 'It'll be you next,' to the oldest attendee at a funeral.

Obviously when a twenty-year-old says they don't want kids, it's implicit that they mean *until I'm older*. Yet everyone responds as if they meant right now, like they're turning down dessert, saying, 'Oh no I couldn't,' only in this case you don't pat your belly to show it's full, but rather to keep it empty. And if you want kids but your partner doesn't, you can't really offer the age-old 'What if we share one?' and ask for two spoons.

No one said, 'Oh, you will,' when I told them I didn't want children. Instead, they said, 'Oh, *she* will.' That's what they expect of my life. That eventually my girlfriend will want a child, because that's what women do once they're bored of shoes and handbags, so instead of ending the relationship so we can both pursue our individual desires, we'd enter into a 1950s compromise in which she gets the gift of my biological baby in exchange for me playing golf every day and smoking a million cigars instead of changing a nappy. Even now, if I say we don't want kids, the first question is, 'Does your girlfriend want them?' Oh, I haven't asked. I didn't think about her. The other part of the 'we' was actually the cat. *We* don't want kids, and that's two against one, so unlucky, darling, you're on your own.

All three of us have held firm, in fact. Despite reaching the age we're supposed to panic at. If, for a moment, I felt the brief twang of being left behind when I noticed all my friends' Mother's Day posts on Instagram no longer featured photos of their mothers, but photos of their wives, that quickly dissipated when I considered the prospect of having to spend the next ten years referring to my girlfriend as 'Mummy'. The only thing I truly envy about my friends who are parents is the absolutely flawless excuse to not attend things that is the ever-unprovable 'childcare issues'. If it wasn't immoral to bring a person into the world purely to use them as a get-out clause, I'd do it in a heartbeat.

That's not to say we're complete outliers. Childlessness is becoming increasingly trendy, in the same way having parents who are still together is now 'cringe'. Fewer and fewer people are having children. In fact, according to the *Guardian*, the number of women reaching thirty child free has increased by around 270% since 1971. There's lots of speculation as to why this might be, from labelling younger generations self-absorbed, to suggesting an increase of career opportunities for women has given them something to focus on other than licking a bit of tissue to rub on a toddler's cheek. Doomsayers think most childlessness is accidental, that this workforce change, coupled with the increasing living costs, means women can't afford to 'take a break' from work until it's biologically too late. That raising a child in a house-share with four others is far from ideal, having to label the lunchables so your forty-year-old flatmate doesn't take them to work. But given that several countries have attempted to alleviate these pressures with financial incentives, literally paying citizens to have children, and it still hasn't moved the needle, it's safe to say in a lot of cases, being child-free is a choice more people are making. It's the new must-have summer accessory: spare time.

Unfortunately, people don't see it that way. You get to a certain age without kids and people think you're weird, assuming you're either swingers or the victims of some sort of ovarian tragedy. At the core of it, you're at least considered selfish for arrogantly dying out, pulling the ladder up behind you, refusing to let a new generation join in on the world. Some will even ask, 'Why not?' once they're satisfied they won't change your mind, and most people who have chosen to remain child-free will throw reasons out to try and justify such a thing, as if that were necessary. 'Having kids is bad for the environment,' they say, as if importing cocaine isn't. 'Having children is a luxury,' their next best option, as if importing cocaine isn't. And try telling a new mum covered in custard at 7 a.m. that she lives a life of luxury, while you can go to the cinema whenever you want. MacBooks are a luxury too, and there's no way they'll eventually pay for themselves by becoming Kylian Mbappé. The excuses carry no weight.

Why do I need a reason to not do something? 'Why not?' is a stupid question when the consequences are so enormous. That's why I never answer it. Surely the actual question is 'Why?' *Why* have kids? Because you're supposed to? Because everyone else does? Because you don't find the airport experience stressful enough? Because you've run out of series to watch and your brain is starting to fill the silence with slightly too honest concerns about your marriage? What do you mean, *why not*? You might as well say, 'Why *not* play Russian roulette? It's something to do, and it only *maybe* destroys your life.'

I do understand the urge to reproduce is biological. That it's hormonal. Evolutionary. All fancy terms for 'impossible to explain with words'. Just like we don't need to explain why we don't want kids, we shouldn't have to explain why we do. And yet, some people do exactly that with all sorts of answers as nonsensical as our own. What follows is a break-down of reasons for having children I've either been told to my face or overheard on reality TV, and why their supposed virtue doesn't hold up for one second.

#1 So You've Got Someone to Look After You When You're Older

Breeding free healthcare. Spawning your own personal nurse on a zero-hours contract. Future-proofing your own incon-tinence with someone who didn't even ask to be alive. If that isn't more selfish than not having a child, I don't know what is. Not to mention how short-sighted it is, given the advance-ments in AI. You won't need your poor middle-aged daughter to come and spend her forty-five minutes of free time at your side when you're 90: there'll be robots for that. And I know everyone hates this idea, because they picture a weird, stiff, silver block-man who clatters when he moves, but at least he can't roll his eyes when you're not looking and fake an emer-gency text to leave early. And that's not what future robots are. By this stage, they will look, sound and move exactly like people. Maybe you'll even be able to get one made to look like your daughter. No one should be having a child just to have someone to wipe their arse in fifty years' time out of some sense of resentful obligation. Change this reason to 'On the Off-Chance My Child Invents the Nan-Bot 3000' and I'll bump it up to acceptable.

#2 To Carry on Your Family Name

Carrying on the family name made sense in the days before Wikipedia and Facebook. Now people are better known by online identities, like BoobMan69, or saved in someone's phone as 'Dave Uni'. No one cares about anyone's actual name. Who do you think you are anyway – Henry VIII? That guy was obsessed with carrying on his family name, and half the world don't even know it isn't a number. Very few people actually care about this one any more, but those who do are some of the most insane (see: posh) little freaks (see: posh) around, creating an actual life for the sole purpose of continuing their own legacy and labelling anyone who doesn't as 'self-absorbed'. Jesus Christ. In fact, good example. Jesus didn't have anyone to carry on his family name and he's got the most famous legacy of anyone! If you care about reputation, surely having a child with your name is an enormous risk. Would Christianity still be a thing if there was a Duncan Christ out there today cat-calling waitresses and pissing on war memorials? If you really want to protect your family name, be nice and die childless.

#3 To Save the Human Race

All right, no one actually says this. Yet. Consider this one a prediction. As populations decline and we begin to see the impact that has on societies, people will start painting themselves as superhero figures, saving the world with sperm. To put it simply, if fewer people have babies, there are fewer babies to grow up and potentially have babies of their own, meaning even fewer kids in the next generation to also grow up to potentially have kids, and so on, leading to the slow spiralling of the human race as a whole. Suddenly, being one of the few who *is* having children is an act of easy heroism. And nothing appeals to people more than claiming something they were already going to do anyway was actually altruistic. A bit like peddling the idea that having children is bad for the environment, when in truth I can't be arsed.

#4 For Religious Reasons

Supposedly some religions encourage their superfans to reproduce, despite the fact God is literally an absentee father. 'Omnipresent' is the lamest excuse in the book. 'I *was* at your football practice, I'm literally everywhere.' Yeah, you're everywhere until we ask you for a favour, then it's straight to voicemail. The fact his hype-men, vicars, make you call *them* 'father' feels like outsourcing to me, or a stepdad trying too hard. Clearly, your beliefs are your beliefs, but if you're looking for a book to follow to the letter, may I recommend *You'll Like It When You Get There* by Rhys James.

#5 To Have a Mini Version of Yourself

What, like Ant and Dec? Do you have any idea how narcissistic that is? I don't know why no one bats an eyelid at this sentiment when referring to reproduction, given how insane we'd all find it if the 'mini you' wasn't a blood relation. Maybe the most prominent character in all of fiction to create a mini version of themselves is Dr Evil. That name again, Dr *Evil*. Now, I don't know exactly what he was like, I've only seen bits of his films, but on a surface level he doesn't strike me as a decent fellow. Or a family name I'd necessarily want to carry on. In reality, this justification actually means, 'I'd like to dress someone up in little tiny versions of the clothes I wear and walk around like mismatched twins.' If that's what you want, your only options are to either have a child or become a national treasure with your own Saturday night ITV format. I know which I'd prefer.

#6 In Pursuit of Meaning

There's the underlying judgement some parents have of non-parents, that their lives lack meaning. That continuing to do whatever you want all the time in service of yourself couldn't possibly have the same depth as dedicating yourself to the education and growth of a new life. It's useful to keep this in mind when one of your parent friends complains about how little sleep they've had, or how sick they are of *Hey Duggee*. 'Yes, but at least you can be awake longer to soak up all that lovely meaning,' I say, like a prick. I am of course aware that life is about purpose. If yours is putting malt loaf into a plastic briefcase, fine. Mine is writing flippant criticisms of exactly that.

#7 The Emotional Fulfilment of Watching Something Grow

Sounds to me like you've never heard of a spider plant. Or a Tamagotchi.

#8 Love

That's what it all comes down to really. Everyone wants love. And when one kind gets boring (partner, football) you've got to mix it up. So how about bringing something into the world that's forced to love you unconditionally for fear you'll stop feeding it? It's a difficult invitation to decline, but may I remind you of the simple concept of 'pets'.

OK, that's harsh, and obviously the desire to nurture and protect is innate within most of us, and for some that manifests in raising a child. Fair play. But ultimately that tells me one thing. The reason you have children isn't specifically for love, to save the world, to carry on your legacy, because God told you to, so that life isn't pointless, or even some noble pursuit like the survival of the car seat industry. In some cases it's not even because it's the done thing. It's because you *want to*. Pure, unbridled 'want'. There's no need to apply logic to something illogical. If it's a calling, then call it a calling. And in doing so, there's your answer to 'why not?' I haven't received the call.

I do feel paternal. I love when people come to me for advice or mentorship. I love knowing I would take a bullet for the cat, not that I can ever imagine a situation in which that is necessary. Maybe an overreaction to her pushing a remote off a table? I'm just not sure feeling paternal is exclusively reserved for fathers. Teachers, for example, presumably feel some level of parental instinct, in between the inevitable murderous rage they're forced to squash down several times a day. Surely that's why you get into teaching? The combination of wanting to nurture and develop the next generation, while still getting summers off. To not have children isn't to close yourself off from them, in the same way not drinking alcohol doesn't shield you from its presence. You still enjoy all the spoils of everyone else getting pissed and slurring on about what a shame it is that you don't get to feel what they feel. But you also get to wake up to a morning that doesn't involve dioralyte or Bluey Live.

Ultimately, everything is selfish. Even selfless acts make us feel good. So yes, maybe not wanting children could be considered self-absorbed. But maybe that's fine. Surely it's better to not have a child if I know I'm too selfish to do it, rather than have a kid and be unable to earnestly dedicate all my energy to them. And isn't that choice the most selfless of all? Did you see how I spun that? Like I say, nothing's more appealing than claiming something you were already going to do anyway was actually altruistic.

Or maybe I simply don't suit fatherhood. I'm not sure anyone's born to be a dad, but if that were possible, then my brother would've come out of the womb sneezing too loudly and turning the heating down in the ward. My sister-in-law too, the most exuberant bundle of permanent 'great vibes' going. Not a requirement to be a parent, but arguably a gap in my CV. They both make parenting look so natural. But it's just not me. I don't *feel* like a father. Man, I *feel* like an uncle. A sentence which would've made a far creepier Shania Twain chorus.

Of course there are things I'm afraid of missing out on by

not having children. And not just practical things, like learning how to zip up a coat from the wrong side while crouching, or how to press 'next episode' on an iPad on the back of my own seat while driving.

I want to lift my child up on my bicep in a swimming pool, convincing them I'm the strongest man in the world when really they don't understand physics, and then refuse to explain it, because appearing strong to them is worth more than a Year 6 science lesson.

I want to meet my daughter's boyfriend, for some reason furious and mistrusting of him for the mere crime of loving the same thing I love but in a different way, slowly being won round to his charms until I start to love what *she* loves in a different way, him, and see the whole thing from his perspective.

I want to miss every single one of my child's big sports games due to 'business', only to finally turn up at the championship match unannounced and have them spot me in the crowd, my presence now meaning more than if I'd been coming all along, like Mum. Then, when they inevitably miss out on the trophy, turn their disappointment to pride with some incredibly sage words about intent and the bravery to even try.

For a navel-gazing, past-obsessed introspective like me, it is incredibly emotionally appealing to get to see the world again through someone else's eyes. As an uncle, I get limited snapshots and anecdotal evidence of this, rather than the constant revelations that come with watching over someone at all times, like a mum, or an eagle. The thing most likely to make me cry in any given situation, be it reality or fiction, is pride. Real, visceral, emotional pride. Parent to a child, child to a parent, sibling to sibling, friends, anything. A bit of earnest pride and I'm gone, drowned in a pool of my own tears, which is probably the most preferable of all of your own fluids to drown in. People always say you don't know real love until you have a child of your own, and it never rings true to me. If they told me you don't know true pride until you have a kid, that might sell it. Sure, I can be proud of my nieces. But will I ever truly feel like Judy Murray does for exactly one of her sons? No one cares who Andy Murray's uncle is.

It has always annoyed me when someone younger than me has told me they're proud of me. Especially if they're a stranger. 'You're not proud of me, kid,' I'd mutter to myself, 'you *respect* me, for I am your elder.' But when I think about having a child, and that child becoming proud of me, and how much that absolutely does me in, I understand pride on an upward trajectory, and I feel a faint calling to fatherhood for the first time in my life.

#9 So That Someone Will Be Proud of You

Without a doubt the bleakest of the lot. Probably don't act on this.

There are other things I'll be sad to miss out on even past the important school years. Frankly, I want to be fifty-five years old and have an adult son or daughter, but I don't want to do any of the work that gets me there. And unfortunately you can't adopt 25-year-olds.

It's a moment in life that has always most appealed to me. Popping to the pub over the holidays and having my own child buy me a pint. Likely with money I've given them. Smugly telling them that every song they like is actually a cover as they disappointedly inform me all those 'news stories' I keep sharing are clickbait. The brief in-between where they're not my child any more, but my peer, before I tip over the other side and end up becoming *their* child. I've loved having that experience as the younger party, so I know I'd love it as a parent too. And yes, I am aware this all sounds like I'm saying I want to get to middle age and still have some cool young people to drink with, but I refuse to pop a number on that and add it to the sad reasons list. This is much deeper. It's the subtle shifting of roles, the beckoning in of a new lead generation, that holds so much more significance when you can witness it first-hand, having had a proper part to play in it all. I don't want children, but I envy what my friends seem to be learning from theirs. I envy what my parents must've learned from me. Both existentially and practically. I mean, if not for me, my mum's iPad would still be a coaster.

There is of course no guarantee of this kind of mutually respectful adult relationship, and perhaps the main thing I'm glad to be missing out on is the Inevitable Projecting of All The Things I Wish My Parents Did or Didn't Do for Me™. It's a classic, isn't it? Parenting through the lens of your own upbringing, forgetting that your child is not a young you, that the world around them has changed. But that wouldn't stop me. My parents always encouraged me to pursue whatever interests I liked, and didn't force me to do anything for longer than I wanted. Of course, this helped inspire a future career in the arts, as I was allowed to grow at my own pace and do things on my own terms. Great. But from a financial perspective, I am fucking livid that they didn't drag me to an open Harry Potter audition when I was ten.

Why didn't my dad make me take 100 free kicks before I was allowed dinner? Why couldn't they force me to have piano lessons until my fingers bled? Did they not envisage a future with free-to-play pianos in every big train station? I don't wish I was a pianist, or a set-piece specialist, or an actor being accused of being 'ungrateful' to the controversial author who created my breakthrough character. But I do resent the fact I possess none of these skills because I was allowed to let my own laziness win out. Thus, as a parent, it would be a constant battle between my better judgement and my inner 'King Richard', demanding the midwives give us an early check-out so we can immediately commence Project Mozart-Beckham-Grint.

In fact, even writing this chapter about not wanting children is part of a long-term strategy. If I were to ever have children, they would surely read this and develop the sort of complex that breeds a life-long need to demonstrate their value to me, AKA the 'Logan Roy' technique. Fast forward a few mentally traumatic decades, and my methods have just created the world's first Nobel-prize-winning trillionaire.

Apparently these days parents are discouraged from saying 'well done' when handed a drawing by their child, and not simply because drawings by children are often rubbish. Doing so teaches them to seek external validation, which can lead to dangerous habits, such as being obsessed with pride. Or trying to make rooms full of strangers laugh. Instead, what you're supposed to say is, 'How do you feel about it?' Which, through the lens of an adult who grew up in a 'well done' world, is possibly the most insulting response imaginable, second only to, 'Are you sure that you're OK?'

Asking someone how they feel about their own work *is* the answer to how you feel about it. Kids aren't stupid. Coming off-stage after one of my early gigs, I saw a comedian I looked up to in the green room. 'I enjoyed that,' he said, which meant the world to me, and was exactly the sort of encouragement I needed. 'Thanks,' I replied, 'I'm so glad.' 'No,' he frowned, 'I said, "Did you enjoy that?" '

As if that passive-aggressive question wouldn't burn on its own without the added backstory of mishearing it for the exact opposite sentiment, the fact he felt the correction was necessary still smarts. So don't tell me a better society this way beckons.

With my nieces, I speak to them like they're adults. Not adults who have just come off-stage in Leek in 2010. But adults all the same. I would never say, 'How do you feel about that?' to an adult, unless I was trying to jinx a therapist. What I would say, tongue-in-cheek, is, 'I can do that better.' That's right. Instead of an outdated 'well done', forcing children to seek the approval of others, I go with the far more cutting 'that's rubbish', training them to feel like nothing's ever good enough. With enough of a glint in your eye and a wry grin, I find this approach can actually lead to an extra layer of fun. If a child does something and you say, 'Very good,' or, 'Do you like it?' then the moment is finished. Work complete and acknowledged, on to the next thing. If you say, 'Yeah, watch this then,' and do the exact jump-spin they've just done, they come back with something even more impressive to try and one-up you. Repeat the process and you really start to get somewhere silly, so long as everyone involved knows it's all for a laugh. Including you.

This is my method, and it's served me well. But, crucially, only as an uncle. If my technique with kids were to be put under the microscope of a broadsheet critic, I imagine they'd call it: 'Disarmingly obtuse, able to wring more from his flying visits than many manage in a full nursery term. A masterclass in bit-part parenting, without a hint of condescension, surely signifying the death of participation-medal culture once and for all.' But apply my same instinctive methods as an actual father, and suddenly it becomes: 'Perhaps the most damaging thing for children's smiles since Sunny Delight, Rhys's ruthless parenting approach borders on the transparent brutality of a beauty pageant mom trying desperately to satisfy the youth they still feel so short-changed by.' In either case, three stars.

Context is everything. So being an uncle, and just an uncle, is what suits me best. It's the perfect cheat code for paternal feelings, with none of the responsibility. There is no better role in the world than being an uncle. The kids are always excited to see me, because I've never told them off or made them do anything they don't want to. Not my job. I'm there to be silly, to be jumped on, to teach new tricks and be shown old ones, and the second anyone gets hungry or tired or both and the tears begin, Nurse Dad turns up to relieve me of my duties. Perhaps instead of offering couples money to have children to solve the potential population crisis, we should simply be encouraging them to become uncles and aunts instead? Something to think about.

There's a mentorship you can't get from your parents, because you're too close to them, that a wise old outsider can offer instead, like a talking tree or a voice in the clouds. I always picture it like the movies: a big grown-up sitting next to a small kid on some steps, throwing rocks at the ocean, shot from behind, as I explain that no one really knows what they're doing, that even grown-ups are making it up as they go along. Directed by Richard Linklater. And obviously I'm aware that barring some sort of catastrophic tragedy in the immediate family, this opportunity rarely goes to the uncle. Uncles are either weird alcoholics you don't want to go near or sacrificial clowns who buy loud birthday presents. You're either Rab C. Nesbitt or you're an inflatable-tube man outside a car wash. Neither of those are top of the life-coach list for a nine-year-old girl.

'Uncle' is in desperate need of a rebrand. I mean, it literally sounds like 'uncool'. Even picturing an uncle, and one we know nothing about – a completely blank, innocent, default video game character uncle – I am unfortunately imagining a nonce. Sort of grey ponytail and glasses, wearing mostly mustard and brown clothing that smells of cigarettes. Why? None of my uncles look like this. And almost all of my friends are uncles. Why do aunts get the luxury of being seen as sweet old cooks, posing with rolling pins and making frozen Yorkshire puddings, while uncles are exclusively pictured as perverts?

When I was a young teenager, refusing to commit to any kind of hobby or goal, while simultaneously phoning-in school and constantly being reprimanded for wasting my own potential, one hero stood tall. My parents did the classic parent move of having a serious word with me regarding my mock exam results and bleating on about the future. But in the distance stood an outsider who knew this method would never work. The future is an intangible prospect. As far as a teenager is concerned, it isn't really there. Even as an adult, every time you eat a McDonald's or drink nine pints, you are ignoring the future's existence. So trying to make me believe a B in geography was going to one day be in the textbook of my own life under the heading 'Events Leading Up to the Shittest Adulthood Imaginable' was a fruitless tactic.

What a kid needs is either immediate threats (you can't have pudding if you don't finish your broccoli) or actual incentives (I'll buy you this toy if you shut the fuck up). That's where my aunt comes in. One summer, with the whole family round, and the topic of conversation turning to my own reluctance to participate in life and all its offerings, my aunt, buoyed by my uncle, chose to shun the other adults' backwards views and drag us all into the modern world, offering me the princely sum of £500 on the completion of a few tasks: matching my predicted GCSE results, doing guitar lessons for one year, continuing to train with the local under-16s football team until the end of the season.

Now. We're. Talking. How can I be expected to do things for the love of them, when they're not things I love? This is the real world, baby, I need to be paid for my manual labour (playing substitute right back for a Hertfordshire boys' team and matching the legal requirement of being educated). This is what having a niece or nephew is all about! Alternative methods. A sideways approach. Something you could never do as a parent or people would whisper when you walked past them. Give half a grand to a child.

I was shown the light by those who came before me and now I must lead by the same example. This is the real circle of life. Wisdom passed down from aunt and uncle to niece and nephew, repeated ad infinitum. Except from my other aunt and uncle, who I always thought were a bit weird for never having kids.

You don't know you're truly ready to become an uncle, it sort of just happens. But once it's begun, and you find yourself in the swing of it all, you realise that actually this was a calling. It's exactly what I'm made for. I was born to be avuncular. I'm not Judy Murray, sat in the players' box, wielding my own sacrifice in every celebratory fist pump. I'm Keith Erskine, Andy Murray's uncle, who got in trouble for tweeting the crying laughing emoji when it was announced Novak

Djokovic would miss the French Open due to injury. I'm not my parents, dangling adult unemployment as some sort of threat as if 'not working' isn't the best-case scenario to a teenager. I'm my auntie, offering cold hard cash incentives for doing a few hobbies.

When the time comes, and my nieces enter their inevitable reluctant teenager phase, I'll be there on the sidelines ready to step in. Not cheering them on. Not putting any pressure on them. But tweeting insults about their rivals, and holding up my debit card. This is where all the money I save on Roblox can go. And the best part is, if they're anything like me, they still won't bother actually doing any of it, and I'll never even have to pay them.

The Jungle VIP

They say that on your deathbed, it's the things you didn't do that you regret the most. Well, obviously. On your deathbed, you're not too hung up on the idea of consequences or shame, are you? Your life is about to end, that's why it's called a deathbed. Naturally your mind goes to: 'I should've been more honest! I should've asked out Jenny from work!' In the real world, when the next chapter isn't eternal nothingness, your mind quite reasonably offers you the flowchart options. 'Be more honest? Ask out Jenny from work? Both potentially lead to a meeting with HR. Do neither.'

Ideally, I won't be faffing about with existential pontification when it's all about to be over. I'd still like to die old, but hopefully get hit by a bus or strangled by my robot carer, desperately grappling for purchase on my flappy gooseneck. 'I should've done more with my life instead of working so much!' Yes, but you couldn't, could you? Capitalism is the constant promise that if you work enough, you can eventually not work at all and focus on doing whatever you want instead, but that promise is delivered upon so late you no longer have the energy. That's the scam. Very few people beat it, and those who do are born rich or live in the woods. If I do have a deathbed, I won't regret things I didn't do. If I regret anything, it'll be the things I did do. Like climbing into that 'death' bed, for a start. What an enormous error of judgement.

The reality is, it's very difficult to make decisions. That's why we often absolve ourselves of all responsibility for them, by flipping a coin, or asking a friend's advice. Or, more sub-consciously, by copying other people. Either in the broad sense, by following traditional life milestones, hitting inevitable checkpoints laid out for you by everyone who has come before, or copying other people in the more specific sense, by copying just one guy. I opted for the 'one guy' method.

When I was younger and desperate not to stand out, I became a social chameleon, acting like the people in whichever social group I currently resided, able to mix it up at the drop of a hat. We all do that to an extent. Maybe you up the syllable count when hanging out with your university course mates, lest they mistake you for a thicko. Perhaps you use a few of the less offensive outdated terms here and there around the 'football' lads, so they don't think you're a journalist. The biggest problem comes when two of these worlds collide, and your secret identity is exposed to the other. It's what makes weddings and stag dos so complicated. How many best-man speeches have you heard that have made you think, 'Really? Anthony? Did *that*?' We are different people to different people. I'm convinced it's why so many young men struggle to introduce their girlfriend to their friends. It's not through a lack of commitment, but from a fear of revealing what charlatans they are, spineless Death Eaters swallowing the identity and gobbling up the cadence of the nearest alpha without even realising. Once there's an audience who know the real, vulnerable you, you can't help but watch yourself from above too, and cringe at the GCSE drama performance you're currently doing.

As you get older and lay out your stall, these situations become more welcome. They certainly did for me, at least.

Even if you're not a particularly individualistic person, the amalgamation of personalities you've collected should be from a large enough pool no one could ever identify the original sources, and you've somehow mixed them all into a unique cocktail you've forgotten the ingredients of. Like most cocktails, this gives you the illusion of confidence. Primarily, a confidence that you are unique, and that's a good thing. No longer desperate to act like everyone else to make the evening go smoother. Happy to be yourself and ruin everyone's night. That's what growing up is. And like most cocktails, it seems to take for ever.

It's not so easy to be yourself at 16, when you don't know who that is. For me, that was the first year of Sixth Form, when all the snarky rudeboys I'd been mimicking had departed at the end of Year 11, to pursue a life of nightclub promotion and unexamined trauma. This left me with a new standard of peer to look up to, which came in the form of Harry in the year above. Head Boy, universally liked, academic, cool, good at football, funny. But crucially – not pretending to be from a different catchment area. He wore his intelligence and interests proudly, while the previous gang wore Nike TNs and knock-off Burberry caps unconvincingly. He was willing to acknowledge that we were growing up in the Home Counties, not Blazin' Squad. He was open-minded and keen to broaden his horizons. He wasn't scared of what other people thought of him. Suddenly I was inspired to be the same. Having spent years trying to be like other people, it dawned on me that happiness lay in being completely authentic. Just like Harry was. So I spent the next two years doing the same. By which I mean copying Harry. Being his authentic self.

And what had he done? Well, the previous year he had

been on a school excursion for four weeks during the summer holidays to Tanzania, climbing Mount Kilimanjaro. So when the opportunity presented itself to spend *my* four-week summer holiday in Borneo, climbing Mount Kinabalu, how could I say no?

Anyone who knew me found this prospect to be absurd. I had never even hinted at having a sense of adventure. At the end of a week-long primary school trip to Weymouth, I was rewarded with a miniature trophy for 'trying new things'. The 'new things' in question being one new thing: shepherd's pie. And people say schools have gone too soft.

Exactly one summer earlier than the proposed Borneo expedition, I celebrated my respectable but not mind-blowing GCSE results with a trip to Reading Festival. Most of my friendship group were heading to Newquay, but fearful of quite how much harder it would be for *me* to deceive the bouncer of beachfront Walkabout that I was eighteen, I opted for the safer, less policeable option of smuggling a few cans into a tent bag, with one other mate, and some friends of friends. Even the festival experience was extreme by my standards, and I was warned by my family about the very real possibility I would find it 'too much'. But when you're a teenager desperately trying to act like your slightly tougher friends, it's easy to convince yourself your parents only know the old you, that they're morons stuck in the past who need a wake-up call. Time to face it, bozos, your son is a grown-up now, and he's got a bucket hat, a packet of Rizla and the lyrics to Jamie T's 'Sheila' memorised start to finish. Get used to it.

Within about forty-five seconds of being at Reading Festival, I found it too much. As a sensory experience, it was like nothing I had ever witnessed, heard or smelled. There's a very specific stench of alleyway garbage that's been pissed on that takes me right back to the anxiety attack of arriving at that festival. To this day, the smell of bonfire smoke combined with any bright colour makes me say, 'This is like Reading Festival,' out loud to people who look at me like I'm Mark Corrigan. 'This is like everything. This is like *fun*,' they retort, and I bluff that that's what I meant.

Festivals to me are effectively the worst version of everything. Do you want to watch a music gig, but outdoors, where the band can't do any proper set design or lighting, and the audience aren't their actual fans? Would you like to have a pint, from an unchilled keg that's been rolled up a hill, and served in a plastic cup your friend will later urinate in and throw into a crowd? How about a hotel room, but instead of walls and plumbing and privacy, it's made of fabric that can't withstand a heavy sigh, is too shallow to stand up in, and your bed is the ground? What about a toilet that's a hole in a phone box and has been used by 60,000 people with hangovers in the past four hours? People always say, 'But you see so many bands in one weekend!' I guess that explains the pills, then. It's all for efficiency.

I have since performed in Reading Festival's comedy tent, and every time I do, all the other comedians complain that it's full of sixteen-year-olds. And it is. That is who it is for. And yet somehow, when I attended at sixteen, I felt completely out of place. Festivals still disgust me but remain one of the main earners in the comedy calendar, so I frequently have to swallow my anxiety as I walk through them to the safety of a backstage teepee.

On the first night of Reading Festival 2007, with everyone in bed at 3 a.m., I left the tent for a piss in the nearby trench. (Read that sentence again if you're a festival lover and tell me I'm wrong for hating them.) In my haste, I made the most schoolboy festival error there is. I did not take notice of where our tent was. We had put a flag on top of it so we'd be able to find it in the rabble, but much like the ribbon-on-the-suitcase trick, if everyone has the same idea, you're no easier to find on the carousel. We should've been the only tent without a flag. Harder to find from a distance, but at least you know you won't be walking in on some strange unwashed shaggers when you do arrive. Instead, I wandered around semi-clothed and semi-aimlessly for what felt like hours, post-piss, in the days before adequate phone torches, desperately seeking either my temporary home or a single bar of phone signal. In general, the rule in Britain is: if you can see a stinging nettle, you're not getting 4G. Especially in 2007, when the first-ever iPhone had just been released, and even if you did have one, there was no way you'd risk it at a festival. These were the days of Sony Ericsson, when one full charge would last the entire weekend and you'd keep a tenner under the battery for emergencies. There was no 4G on this thing even if you weren't in a field. All we had was WAP, the original kind, used for checking football transfers, rather than the more recent Cardi B kind, used for making Piers Morgan angry. I couldn't drop a pin and find my tent, unless it was an actual pin, and that's harder to find than a flag.

I was completely lost, overwhelmed and beginning to panic as I faced the prospect of wandering around until the sun came up, avoiding the festival-hardened all-nighter freaks, with their illegal roll-ups, European dance music and, as it was 2007, trilbies. I spent so long as a teenager trying to seem older than I was, but the second I was faced with a crisis, where everyone surrounding me seemed so natural and at home, I crashed back down to the reality that I was still a child, and should never have been allowed to get into this mess. Pathetically, I found the tent within the hour. When I woke up the next morning I phoned my mum to pick me up. She refused.

I had never done anything that could remotely pass as preparation for a trip like Borneo. My holidays as a child often involved road trips, but there was very little for me to think about, except memorising Robbie Williams lyrics in the back of hired beamers, until we arrived at another beautiful Massachusetts national park to take disposable photos of. I didn't grow up in a rich family, just a spendthrift one. On one trip to Disneyland, my dad surprised us all with an airport transfer in the most needless stretch limousine you've ever seen. Nothing was more jarring than a pale, British family of four, alighting their economy flight, grabbing their Argos suitcases and loading them into a stretch limo, in which we spent the entire time asking the driver which famous people he'd driven, becoming the first limo passengers in history to watch the partition window slide up so the *driver* could have some privacy. Obviously these days, the limo experience has been sullied by hen parties and teenage prom-goers, bringing the image down a tax bracket with their shrill screams from the sunroof or squashing in so many guests they end up with less space than they'd have in a normal car. My family were the original limo ruiners, making them uncool all on our own, taking photos with the driver as if *he* was the celebrity, and pressing the intercom to check if the Dr Peppers in the mini fridge were included in the hire price. Ballers!

There would be no limos in Borneo, but I didn't need one. I had had my limo experience, and I was ready for something new. It may have been daunting, and I may have lacked the skill set or willpower to go through any kind of hardship whatsoever. But what I did have, in spades, was a desire to be Harry.

And so I grew a sense of adventure from nowhere, and preached it to all the mindless sheep who didn't have one. 'There's a whole world out there, actually,' I'd tell them, smugly. 'It's not going to come to you. There are tons of other cultures doing things differently to us, and maybe you'll get some perspective, if you care enough to look for it?'

As it turns out, I didn't care enough to look for it. At least not in the right places. True to form, at the last minute, I bottled the chance of a lifetime and dropped out of the Borneo trip.

Some would call it growth. At least I'd done it in advance this time, instead of phoning my mum from the top of Mount Kinabalu to ask her to pick me up, having wandered off from base camp for a midnight piss. But most would call it wussing out. When I had initially told my mum and dad about the trip, it felt like I was coming out as gay to parents from the 1950s. 'This isn't you,' they pleaded, 'you're just going through a phase.' But when I sat them down to tell them I was no longer going to Borneo, it was like I was coming out in 2024, and they responded like the modern, progressive parents they are. 'We know, Rhys. We've *always* known.'

There was no real moment of realisation that I was going to bail on my adventure, just a mounting sense of dread. The trip drew nearer and something completely hypothetical suddenly came into focus as something real. Borneo felt like a risk, and I wasn't a risk-taker. So, despite having already bought the oversized hiking backpack, and paying a non-refundable £500 deposit, which could've so easily been earned from my aunt by simply participating in society but was instead saved up over several birthdays, I squashed any hope of being Harry and opted instead to join the rest of my school year in Kavos, sharing 'fishbowls' on 'the strip' and 'failing' to 'kiss anyone'.

As far as sliding doors moments go, this is without a doubt the second biggest of my life. The biggest, of course, was watching the film *Sliding Doors*. If I hadn't done that, I wouldn't look at everything through a lens of 'what might've been' and I might be able to actually get on with my life. And they say it's the things you didn't do that you regret the most.

Going to Kavos wasn't very 'me' either, of course, it was simply the easier option. And I bloody loved those. That's who I was. We can just thank the Lord I'd depleted my savings of its last £500, or I'd probably have spent it on a limo from the airport.

Many of my peers who did go to Borneo were encouraged to keep travel diaries so they could look back in years to come on what a life-enriching experience they were privileged enough to have. No one suggested doing the same in Kavos. If anything, they pushed for discretion, which is probably why they all tried to drink away their memories in real time.

Thankfully, as someone who was forced to write holiday diaries as a child so I could remember Universal Studios and needlessly long taxis, I can draw on experience to talk you through the details of my expedition to a teenage-party town on the coast of a Greek island. Harrowingly, both the Kavos and Borneo trips occurred at the exact same time, allowing my brain to freely montage what I was doing versus what I could have been doing instead if I wasn't such a wimp, a sort of 'here's what you could've won' for my own future.

Day One: Travel

Alarms wake us before dawn, so we can grab the day by the horns. And make the 05:49 from Harpenden to Luton

Airport Parkway. Bags packed with essentials: swimming shorts, flip-flops, Shockwaves, factor 50, a striped polo shirt I've for some reason bigged-up to my friends as 'the greatest T-shirt I've ever bought', which will prompt them to mockingly ask 'Is this the one?' about everything I wear for the duration of the holiday. I also include some non-essentials: snorkel, a book, condoms.

The group meet at the airport, where we're handed our matching 'lads' holiday' T-shirts: a navy blue number with the words 'Kavos 2008, The Lads' circling an embroidered pint glass. On the back are our nicknames: Smudge, Jonno, PJ, Big Dave, Woody and so on. Mine: *Jonesy*. I have never been called this name in my life. Penguin, Reej, RhysyPoo and Rhysy Baby (something a geography teacher once called me which would've felt wildly inappropriate if we didn't all think she was fit) were all there for the taking. I had been called all of these at some point, even if just by myself on the internet, but not Jonesy. Jonesy is my father. Do I put this T-shirt on and become my dad, like Jim Carrey putting on The Mask? If so, I'm about to be livid that we didn't get to the airport two hours earlier.

Looking round the airport we spot another group of lads with nickname T-shirts, which spirals me into an existential crisis, suddenly hyperaware that there are so few unique experiences in the world, and I've passed up one of my biggest chances to have one by coming *here*. This is quickly replaced with extreme gratitude at my own 'nickname', when one of those lads turns around to reveal he is apparently better known as 'Piss 'n' Shit'. No speculation required for that story. Unless Piss 'n' Shit is his father?

Meanwhile, practical, versatile items are packed into practical, versatile, Borneo-bound backpacks. Trousers that zip off into shorts, mosquito spray, diarrhoea medication, water canteens. A seventeen-hour direct flight is eventually slept off in jungle hammocks, as the group acclimatise to the humidity and culture shock of their new island surroundings.

We've got our own jungle to acclimatise to in Kavos: 'the strip'. An all-but-pedestrianised catwalk of neon-signed bars and fast-food chains, all pumping out what sounds like remixes of the same song. Everyone is British. No. Worse. *Everyone* is from *Harpenden*.

Day Two: Parasites

Hangovers are tested with the 'Poolympics', an obstacle course made up of different-shaped inflatables. The group begin to settle into their new routine: do nothing for eight hours, then all compete for the shower, before getting dressed, gelling our hair and heading back downstairs in the hotel for pre-drinks, at which a child of the family who own the 'hotel' pours Coke from a two-litre supermarket bottle into a plastic cup of cheap vodka for four euros. Our diet is made up exclusively of cheese toasties and chips, and we all play cards while listening to someone's iPod nano, until heading off to the same bars on the strip as the night before.

In Borneo, the team are taught about the ecosystem of the rainforest and the looming threat of deforestation. As if that weren't enough to contend with, parasites ravage the wildlife, reducing the food supplies for mammals within, endangering them further.

The strip has its own parasites to contend with: club reps. You can't walk ten yards without one of these vultures approaching with a made-up drinks offer for the bar behind them. They hound you like charity muggers you can't fob off with claims you're late, or French. 'You can get a cocktail and a shot for five euros each!', 'Jug of WooWoo for ten people, only twelve euros!' We all attempt to negotiate like *Apprentice* candidates, offering outrageous figures back to them. Eventually a single member of the group claims to have found us a great deal of two 'fishbowls' of a drink called 'Headfucker'. With no idea what this means, we follow. It turns out a fishbowl is quite literally a big bowl of liquid, in which you all put a straw and drink consistently until it's finished. The reason it's called a Headfucker is presumably because it forces groups of defiantly heterosexual lads to contend with the fact they are drinking each other's saliva while making prolonged eye contact.

We progress down the strip and into several other bars, but mostly to collect pints of Sex on the Beach before standing around in the street with everyone from school. The girl I love clutches the waist of a boy on a quad bike and disappears into the night.

Day Three: Sealife

Jonno has gone missing. Of course it's entirely possible he has pulled and stayed at someone else's hotel, but he isn't really the type, and there are growing fuzzy accounts of seeing him stumble off to the beach around 4 a.m. We send out a search party when he's still not back by 3 p.m., but while we're out, he turns up at the hotel in last night's clothes and with a huge gash on his leg. He claims he woke up on a rowing boat in the ocean, with no memory of how he got there, or how he got the gash. The group has great fun with his use of the word 'gash'.

In Borneo, it's white-water rafting down the rapids, before a more gentle excursion down the Padas River to their next destination, a family home in a rural village.

Day Four: Family

Until now, the only other people staying at our hotel have been some girls from our school, including the one who officially rejected me three days prior to this holiday. I had issued her a 'me or him' ultimatum and been dumbstruck when it was met with an unheard-of third option: 'neither'. Despite my heartbreak, we had vowed to remain friends, and the best way to do that was clearly to sit near each other by a swimming pool in next to no clothing.

A British family arrive at the hotel. A heavily tattooed mother and father, a four-year-old boy obsessed with watching you go on your phone over your shoulder, and a teenage boy you can tell has at one point shaved a Nike tick into his hair. We invite Shane, the elder of the kids, to join us on our night out. He tells us he'll see us out there, but mostly spends his nights out 'on the rob', nicking cash and phones from wasted holidaymakers. We all admire (see: fear) his honesty.

In Borneo, a local family teach the travelling party to cook Laska and thatch hut roofs from coconut leaves. In return, the expedition crew plant trees and help build jungle trails, before assisting with preparing a village banquet with their newly learned skills.

I spend the afternoon in our hotel badly disguising my hung-over melancholy, eventually asking the source of my heartbreak for a quiet chat. She says she'll come up to my balcony in five minutes. Forty minutes later, she hasn't turned up. I stay to ponder my situation alone for a while, concluding that jumping would probably just break my ankles.

Day Five: Music

For the past few nights, pre-drinks has concluded with the entire group of lads in one hotel room, crowded around a speaker, absolutely belting out a singalong to Panic! At The Disco's 'I Write Sins Not Tragedies', a sort of emo showtune that is brand new to the sporty lads who'd typically favour some 'Nelly and Kelly'. What starts as a semi-ironic tradition quickly becomes a sort of team talk to gee everyone up before heading back to the strip, on which we have been responding to the annoying club reps by singing over their offers and scattering off into the evening.

We bump into our tatted hotel friends outside the most popular bar, Rolling Stone. While catching up on what they've been up to in the forty minutes since we saw them last, Shane pinches my wallet out of my pocket and hands it back to me, in order to demonstrate how easily done it is, like a scam awareness campaign. I'm grateful for the lesson, but I'm terrified of my teacher.

In Borneo, the Brits' hard work is rewarded with an afternoon at the hot springs, before the locals see them off from the village with a cultural dance performance, a thank you for their hard work.

The lads on the strip try to beat the mechanical football challenge, in which you attempt to score penalties against a motorised wooden goalkeeper who is too big for the goal. Jed, who 'would still play for Arsenal if he didn't break his leg' scores, winning two bottles of something they've labelled 'champange' (not a typo). Will can't find his phone.

Day Six: Wildlife

Today's the day to visit the conservation area, a local café called Union Jacks known for curing six-day hangovers with their legendary full English. A home away from home, to protect the least endangered species of all: pissed Brits.

In Borneo, they visit biodiversity hotspot Danum Valley, home to the Bornean orangutan, the pygmy elephant, the clouded leopard and the proboscis monkey. They spend the day investigating the hundreds of endangered species of animals under a rainforest canopy that's older than the Amazon.

We head out to Rolling Stone early, and watch as a familiar-looking man walks over to the DJ booth to whisper something. Suddenly, the DJ announces that Pat Sharp is in the house, and we race over for a photo.

Day Seven: Endurance

A competition is started to see who can stay in the pool for the longest. Thankfully, the pool is in view of a television which is showing the Wimbledon final. I see this as an opportunity to win something sports adjacent, in a group I would otherwise stand no chance of, under the guise of an 'endurance challenge'. Several players, including me, pledge to stay in until the tennis ends, but many fall by the wayside as it goes on to become the longest Wimbledon final in history, lasting four hours and seventeen minutes. By set five, we are all prunes of men, shivering like war veterans. I win, but at great cost, and to little fanfare. It's no surprise the sport I excel at is doing nothing for the longest. I've been training for it my whole life.

One more night out, which involves finally discovering the enormous, thousand-capacity nightclub round a corner we hadn't bothered to venture. It's an absolute metropolis and was exactly what we'd been crying out for while spending our evenings standing around on the strip with other people from our school. The next morning, we return home, facing the enormous uphill battle of having to tell our parents 'all about it'.

In Borneo, they arrive at base camp to prepare for a week-long ascent of Mount Kinabalu. They have three weeks left to go. The adventure is just beginning.

When I arrived home from Kavos, I felt like I was on my deathbed. I didn't regret going, and I still don't in isolation. But I do regret not going to Borneo. I regret the fact that when faced with the fork in the road, with signs pointing to 'Conventional' and 'Adventurous', I of course chose the easiest option. I can't help but wonder if that single decision somehow signed me up for the entirely wrong future. Would I still be the dread-riddled, life-avoiding weasel I am now if I had taken the risk and faced my fears, instead of being lured into the cage of my own comfort zone with 2-for-1 cocktails, slurping obliviously as the door locked behind me for ever? It's a real headfucker.

The following year, when we did an identical trip to Malia, which included all of my friends who had previously gone to

Borneo, I felt the overwhelming sense that I really could have had it all.

You can't avoid consequences by not doing things. In fact, often not doing things has bigger consequences than doing them. Sure, asking out Jenny from work might lead to a tribunal, but not asking out Jenny might kill your one chance at happiness, and surely that's worse?

Of all the things I didn't do as a teenager, and all the things I still haven't done now, the fact I didn't go to Borneo at that formative age nags at me like a Kavos club rep. Followed closely by the fact, on looking at the holiday photos, it turns out I also haven't met Pat Sharp, but someone who looks like him. And if I ever do get the chance to clamber into an actual deathbed, it'll be that I regret the most.

Neighbourhood Listen

Daphne and I bought a house towards the tail end of the pandemic. I call it a house, but it's a maisonette in a block, with its own entrance and a small garden, at the end of which is a shed-office built by the previous owner, now used as a place to play darts when I should be writing this book. The garden is overlooked by an identical block of flats behind it. A balcony runs along the front, which all the upper-storey residents walk along to enter and exit their homes, or scream down to Uber Eats drivers who refuse to come up. The eyeline into our living room from this balcony is so direct, it might as well be a VIP viewing gallery, and a man who has thrice mistaken me for Ed Gamble in Sainsbury's Local stares directly into our flat every single time he leaves his house. Daphne finds this so invasive she's taken to making rude gestures back at him, so apologies to Ed's wife, Charlie – that guy thinks you're a prick.

Unfortunately, I am in the business of being both seen and perceived. By putting myself on-stage I am at the mercy of an audience's judgement, inviting them to see me through their own lens. All performers are, to an extent. But I am at least in some control of what that judgement is. I can't decide if someone else likes me or doesn't, but I can control the 'me' they're voting on, choosing which parts of myself to amplify and which to leave on mute.

In stand-up, I've been accused of not showing enough of myself, prioritising punchlines over vulnerability. Given my job description, it feels odd to slag me off for being too jokey. When my plumber fixes a leaking U-bend, I pay him and say thanks. I don't ask for deeper meaning. 'That's all well and good, Keith, but what about your childhood? Why do you feel the need to stop the leak in the first place? Is it a metaphor for repressing your emotions, or is it like everything else: so your dad will finally love you?'

To finally reveal all my insecurities here in writing, then, is a daunting task. No longer would I have control of the narrative. No more could I twist people's perceptions into what I wanted them to be. The truth would be out. No going back. But as I considered the prospect, and the advance I had been offered, I realised we are all being perceived for who we really are anyway. From all angles, all the time. From people in shops, to strangers on the street. Our families, friends, all perceiving us and forming judgements, as we are about them.

Maybe we control those perceptions too, putting on little social performances until we feel comfortable enough to let go. But what about our neighbours, or the people we live with, who see every version of us including our worst? The stressed, unwashed, hung-over, pyjama'd version we'd prefer to conceal. We can't all be secretly waking up three hours earlier than our partners to put on make-up like *The Marvelous Mrs. Maisel*. Like it or not, no one knows you quite like a housemate.

Some people live alone of course. But I've spent the last twelve years residing in London, where that is only possible if you're in solitary confinement, or finance. London is a cultural behemoth, buzzing with life and inspiration. It is hundreds of unique villages connected by the best transport system in the world. From the wealthiest stoops to the most destitute alleys and everything in between, London is all things to all people. But as a result, it is inhabited by the most diverse range of savages and freaks the world over. And most of them have lived either with or next door to me. When you try to stay at home as much as I do, you need that home to be a sanctuary. It has never once come close.

Before we moved to 'the *Off Menu* aquarium', we spent our pandemic in a tiny attic on the other side of London, living on the same road as Stanley Johnson and a few streets away from Daniel Craig. My entire London living experience, until now, has been in large Victorian houses that have been sliced up into four flats and priced as though you were renting the whole thing. Stanley and Daniel presumably own all of theirs, but you never know, it is London. It was very jarring seeing the prime minister's dad walk around the park during the one hour of exercise a day his own son had permitted us all. And very difficult not to heckle him about his parenting skills.

In the apartment beneath us were a shy Northern lad and his confident American boyfriend. On paper it was the exact sort of odd-couple dynamic that carries a sitcom, and in reality too, as we'd frequently overhear their extremely one-sided arguments coming through the floorboards. Given the mandated isolation of the whole situation, we spent a good few weeks thinking the American may have killed the other one and gone insane, propping up his body to yell at every hour, never getting any response. Thankfully, we saw the quiet one coming back from the shops before we had to call the authorities.

On the ground floor was where the real drama lived, where an on-again-off-again couple soundtracked our lives with a

mixture of screams, both in ecstasy and rage. The front door
to their flat was right next to the main entrance to the building, their bedroom sharing a wall with the foyer, which we
all used to sort out our post. It didn't matter what time you
were coming or going, the shrieks scored your journey at
10 p.m. or 10 a.m. I frequently had to deal with sheepish-
looking delivery drivers, shocked by the noises coming from
inside, that to me had become so commonplace I barely heard
them any more. 'Don't mind her,' I'd say, taking the parcel
out of their hands, 'she just really loves ASOS.'

When they found time between orgasms, they'd have
equally loud rows. Thankfully this never coincided with a
package arriving, or I'd have been telling delivery drivers,
'Don't worry, she just really hates Zara.' We'd sometimes
have to step in, attempting to calm things down to no avail,
until one day, the lady of the house sought refuge in the
American's flat to call the police. Before they could arrive,
her boyfriend fled the scene and didn't return until a week
later.

When we heard him outside her door again, we raced
downstairs to send him away, but when we arrived, we
noticed his hand was slashed and bleeding profusely. It certainly didn't look like he was creating his own excuse to get
out of doing a comedy gig, so we asked what was going on.
He said he needed his wallet back so he could leave for ever.
It took what felt like an age to convince her to hand it over,
all the while his blood was dripping onto the communal
carpet of a building owned by a landlord who hadn't let me
get Sky because the dish on the building's exterior would be
'unseemly'.

A month later, when I received an invitation to self-tape
for a big film, I felt incredibly conscious of our middle-floor

neighbours. A self-tape is an audition that you record your-self at home and send to the casting director via email. It was a complete necessity during lockdown, but as such, meant partners and housemates were often roped into reading the other parts off-screen. The script for this film involved a shouting match between a couple which descends into a bout of actual violence, requiring us to scream in anguish before collapsing to the floor. We got through one take before realis-ing we should probably let the boys downstairs know what we were doing, before in turn realising quite how suspicious that sounded, and abandoning the audition entirely.

Before the attic, we lived in a flat previously occupied by two couples who ran both a pizza delivery service and a bar-bershop out of the same carpeted living room, and clearly reserved no budget for cleaning. The shaggy carpet was matt with either hair or dough or hair in dough. When our land-lord decided to sell the flat only six months after we'd moved in, we weren't as gutted as we might've been, despite how annoying it was having to look for a new home so quickly. After a while on the market with zero viewings, Daphne became suspicious and asked her mum to book in a viewing herself as a ruse. As she was shown around our flat by an unsuspecting estate agent, my mother-in-law by proxy com-plained about the filthy carpets, and assuming this was the reason it wasn't selling, the landlord finally had them profes-sionally cleaned. Eventually he took it off the market and asked us to stay, which I agreed to on the proviso of a signifi-cant rent discount. I played the *Succession* theme tune every time I recounted the tale to anyone.

My first London flat was shared with two friends of mine: a comedian and a YouTuber. We lived in a spacious apartment in a cultural dead-zone of north-west London, above a pernickety woman who tutted so much you'd think she was permanently trying to beckon a cat. There wasn't a thing she didn't tell us off for, from hoovering to taking too long picking up our post from the shared entrance. She waited at her door like a hawk, and often outside ours too, with her ear pressed up against it, on one occasion even barging into our flat to film our toilet, which she was convinced was leaking into hers, despite various handymen informing her this was impossible. A guest once informed me she had come knocking while I had been in the shower, to which I suggested she was probably coming to have a go at me for something. Before I could finish the sentence, there was another knock at the door. It was her. She had been waiting there this whole time. 'I wasn't having a go at you,' she said defensively. 'I was going to warn you that there's a branch on the driveway that could be very danger-ous.' It had all the conviction of someone pretending to have seen *Austin Powers*. 'So . . . be careful to step over it.' She didn't bother us much after that.

I had obviously lived with other men my age at university, but this experience was unique and fraught with some of the most baffling behaviour of all time. Firstly, the comedian, my closest friend Justin, had a habit – nay, routine – of cooking one million onions every morning at 8 o'clock. If you've ever wondered what would make a good alarm clock for a deaf person, the stench of morning onions certainly gets you out of bed, though it doesn't come with a snooze button. His style was to cook an enormous pot of something bolognese adja-cent when he woke up, then leave it on the hob all day, periodically spooning it into his gob throughout the morning, afternoon and evening, with individual slurps of slop for sus-tenance, rather than the more traditional 'three meal' method of every other human being. These days, he'd be hailed as some sort of bio-hacking, cortisol-controlling, age-reversing genius by Steven Bartlett, and get a sponsorship from Huel. Back then I considered him a psychopath. I really can't stress how many onions this guy cooked at 8 a.m. There were so many onions, on more than one occasion I woke up with tears in my eyes. There is no such phrase as 'wake up and smell the onions', and that is because it wouldn't mean 'see the situation for what it is' or 'appreciate what you have', but rather, 'be so depressed you literally cry from the moment you regain consciousness', or at least 'find a new housemate'.

In general, though, I loved this house-share, which is remarkable given how often I woke up crying. The real trouble only began when our third housemate, a generally quiet creative who kept himself to himself, mainly leaving his room to play video games in the dark at 3 a.m., decided it was time to move out, and had to be replaced by a guy neither of us had ever met. A mistake I will never make again.

The entire point of this stranger living with us was to prevent me and Justin from swallowing the rent of the extra room, but we ended up doing just that, as he never paid it, instead sending us long, pleading WhatsApps about how hard times were for him at that moment. One thing to bear in mind, before you brandish me a heartless boomer landlord bastard, is that this man was an amateur musician who had convinced himself he was a professional, and therefore refused to get a day job. He slept until 4 p.m. every day, and then either went off to an open mic or, more often, went to watch a friend do a paid gig so he could ask them to return the favour of his support by buying him pints all night. He was happy to spend money on vinyl records or special edition DVDs of *Sophie's Choice* (despite not owning a DVD player), just not any of his actual obligations. One day, moments after receiving a four-paragraph message about why his rent was late through no fault of his own, I found a receipt under his coat in the hallway. It was from a 'restaurant' he had 'dined' at called Choccywoccydoodah. He had ordered something called 'Chocolate Everything' for £28.

Rent was the least of our worries though. There were plenty of things this guy didn't have: a job, money, talent. But most importantly: a towel. That's right. He didn't own a towel. This wasn't something he bragged about, it's something I uncovered about him after extensive investigation. With Justin enjoying the spoils of the en suite in our room rotation system, I was left to share a bathroom with the new guy, something I wouldn't wish on my worst enemy, which, funnily enough, was him. Among a litany of other issues, the main one was that his occasional showers took for ever. I quickly noticed, however, that despite dedicating an inordinate amount of time to bathing, the water wouldn't be running for long, and he never smelt better than 'unique'. So what was going on in there? Suspicious, I noticed that immediately after a shower, the bathmat, which had been provided by me, would be soaking wet. Not with footprints, but wet enough to suggest he had been using it as an anti-slip mat in the shower itself, or a lilo in the bath. So, to gather data, I removed it from the bathroom.

The next time he had a shower, I went into the bathroom after him once again, like a weird hygiene-based Poirot, or Columbo-de-Toilette. Typically you'd think a bathmat disappearing might prompt a few questions, mostly directed at the guy whose bathmat it is, who you share a bathroom with. But he stayed silent. He did not want to have the bathmat conversation. Instead, a similar degree of wetness had this time been applied to the hand towel. The one by the sink, that you'd use to dry your hands if you washed them after you went to the toilet, which in his case genuinely is an 'if'. Or worse, the one you'd wipe your face on after brushing your teeth. Well, now it was drenched. Clearly, at the very least, used to dry my nemesis's body, but looking like it was used to dry everything that's ever taken on moisture. There was a possibility he was actually showering the towels themselves, rather than his own body. It would explain not just how wet they were, but also why he smelled like that, and why he didn't see the need to possess a towel of his own. But the experiment had to continue. I removed the hand towel from the bathroom.

What would turn up on that bathroom radiator from here on out became increasingly inexplicable. First, a cricket jumper. Soaked to the bone. Rained off. Sure, it looks woolly enough to get you dry, but there surely comes a point where you catch yourself in the mirror drying yourself with your own clothes and think, should I cut down on Chocolate Everythings so I can buy one of the most basic items in the history of human functionality? Clearly not.

I couldn't remove the cricket jumper as it wasn't mine and I desperately didn't want to touch it, but days later, something turned up that saved me having to. On the radiator of the bathroom this time, draped, heavy with the weight of a thousand oceans, was one single glove. A woolly, black glove. You're picturing it, I'm picturing it. We all know what happened. There's no way it's efficient enough to use that glove like a towel by simply holding it in your hands. The only way would be to put the glove on and slowly rub it over your body until you're drip-free – like you're applying fake tan, or impersonating Michael Jackson.

These days I don't have to worry about the bathing habits

of my housemate, barring the fact that being in a relationship with a woman means unsticking clumps of hair from the shower tiles and returning the shower head to an adult height every morning until you die. The big concern with our current situation is the neighbours. The area in general is incredibly noisy, with firework displays that last twenty seconds occurring randomly like some sort of razzle-dazzle smoke signal. Apparently this is a drug thing, but it feels far too flamboyant to exist in that world. I'm HEEEERE, if you want your bag then COME AND GET ME, BOYS! The fly-tipping in the area is also out of control – I once saw an inflated and still full paddling pool. What kind of scenario leads a man to dispose of a paddling pool mid-paddle? A lack of towel? That's preposterous.

We have noisy neighbours in every direction. Above, left, right. Even below, which is concerning, as we live on the ground floor. It's a truth universally acknowledged that anyone living upstairs from you is nocturnal and has the following hobbies: rearranging furniture, ten pin bowling, auditioning for the musical *Stomp*, dropping things. You will wake four times a night in cold sweats from a nightmare about living inside a pool table. Our particular upstairs flat has homed a revolving door of couples who hate each other, eventually breaking up and replacing the din of their arguments with Gotye's 'Somebody That I Used to Know' on repeat. On one occasion I got a knock at the door, and upon opening it, a bedraggled-looking man began walking into my house saying he needed to get something from my garden. I pushed him back onto the doorstep, citing something about not letting the cat out, and asked what the hell he thought he was doing. Barge into my house filming my bathroom once, shame on me . . . He told me his girlfriend had thrown loads of his stuff off their balcony into our garden and he needed to retrieve it. The 'stuff' consisted of a shoe, which I found, and his car key, which I did not. Naturally they moved out, presumably hiring a car to do so, and were quickly replaced by a couple of tap-dancers with a home gun range.

To the left, we have a gaggle of Deliveroo drivers. Is gaggle the right word? Maybe a 'tandem'. I assume they are Deliveroo employees, but they could just be big fans of the merch. For the most part, these guys are no trouble, except from the fact you never see the same one twice. At least six of them live there at any one time, and the faces entering and exiting the house, taking out the bins or picking up their bikes, are always changing. Maybe those big square backpacks are portals? But why would you go through it if it led you to a pokey flatshare in the East End? They have a barbecue every day and are all obsessed with Italian hip hop, which they play at full blast, on a speaker they had installed on the *exterior* wall in the back garden.

One day I was plucking up the courage to ask them to turn it down. They say you either die cool or live long enough to become your former downstairs neighbour. Before going round, for some reason I decided to google the lyrics of the song they kept playing. '*Tradiri mai, tradiri mai,*' the chorus echoed, which, it turns out, means, 'If you ever betray me.' So perhaps it was *Sicilian* hip hop. Suffice to say, I never said a thing, lest I wind up a decapitated head in a Deliveroo backpack.

On the other side lives a large family who seemingly work from home as competing town criers. But town criers who very much disagree on the content of their announcements. They scream at each other all day, in increasingly shrill tones, slamming every door to represent every full stop. Our living room is but a wall away from their living room; our kitchen, their kitchen; our bedroom, their child's bedroom.

Owing to a lack of space in London, properties are necessarily squashed together, but hearing so much of what's going on in the next one makes it feel like we all live in one big, horrifying flatshare. Seemingly, when our block was built they fitted the walls with a ground-breaking technology, which, rather than sound-proofing each individual home, instead amplifies and reverberates every single noise, until it feels like it's happening directly inside your own ear canal. It's not just the screaming, it's literally every single noise. People say 'you could hear a pin drop' to mean something is silent. I could hear a pin drop in my neighbours' house, because the walls are made of megaphones.

The mum of the family spends all day chopping vegetables to the same monotonous rhythm. With my neighbours on the other side playing constant hip hop, this means both my time inside my house and out in my garden are soundtracked by 180 BPM. When their smoke alarm needs batteries, I know as early as they do. It's one thing having to deal with the piercing low-battery bips of your own pointless smoke alarm, which only otherwise exists to taunt you in your most stressful moment, letting the whole street know how shit you are at cooking, as you frantically fan at it with a tea towel like a wartime housewife waving off a naval ship. But to listen to those endless bips, at such inconsistent intervals, prodding into my skull through the walls with no power to do anything about it myself, is absolute torture.

As if that wasn't enough, the six-year-old we share a bedroom wall with has recently set his morning alarm to 4 a.m., despite there being zero evidence he delivers milk for a living, nor any suggestion he's a rise-and-grind hustler selling a course on drop-shipping to other ambitious toddlers. Why does a six-year-old need a morning alarm at all? Let alone the same one as a baker. Somehow the alarm next to his head didn't wake him up for twelve minutes, despite waking me up immediately, a whole brick wall away. It took an alarm *and* us banging on the wall for him to eventually wake up and switch it off. A week later I ordered a smoke alarm battery anonymously to their house. It took a further two weeks for them to use it.

Despite how infuriating this all is, what's even worse than the noise I hear from their side is how much it reminds me of the noises they must've heard coming from ours. I don't have to worry about the usual stuff, like arguments or passionate love-making. We're doing fine, but years of living in the same building as exhibitionists has given us the common courtesy to keep it between us. More, I worry about them hearing the made-up songs I sing to myself all day, the TikToks I laugh at that I'd be ashamed for anyone to witness, the way I speak to the cat. My God, the way I speak to the cat. Plaster a picture of my flaccid dick next to a screen grab of my credit card details on every billboard in central London before you expose a single second of my cat voice. I am a different person when I look at her.

All this is to say, when it's not absolute agony to have the drums played on your brain by the percussion section that is your neighbourhood, it's quite jarring to have the existential bombshell that you too are being heard and perceived at all times, making you self-conscious in the privacy of your own home. So when I say I don't want to come out, know that this is where I'm choosing to be instead. In hell.

I know deep down that one day I simply must escape it all. To find somewhere quiet and remote. To figure out if the voices in my head are even there, or if I am mistaking them for actual voices, right next to my head. Maybe that's why they keep telling me to go to my room and threatening me in Italian?

When you're anxious, people tell you to meditate. But how? Meditation is clearly a privilege of those rich enough to afford a detached house. If I attempted to meditate at any point during my London living experience, I'd be forced to sit cross-legged on the floor atop a pile of hairy pizza dough, my calming deep breaths would fill my nose with the stench of onions, and closing my eyes would give my nemesis the chance to sneak into my room and steal back the bathmat. I wouldn't hear silence; I'd hear the consistent, sharp bips of an uncharged smoke alarm I can't do anything about. I wouldn't feel centred; I'd feel too conscious that onlookers are gaining an unfair perception of Ed Gamble as a Zen master. It just wouldn't work. And when would I find the time anyway? I've got to get to bed. I'm up at 4 a.m. to bang on the wall.

Sex and Other Fears

Everything's easier after the first time. Because everything's daunting before you've tried it. Obviously the world is full of people who throw caution to the wind and just do things, like asking someone out or attempting a backflip, but those people have part of their brain missing, probably from botching said backflip. I relate to these people so little I literally had to look up 'Spontaneous Things to Do' to find examples, and in doing so invented perhaps the most self-defeating Google search since 'alternatives to Google'. But these people do exist. They're in dance classes and paint shops. They Lime bike everywhere and have a different hair colour every month. Their dating profiles claim they like 'trying new things!' And some of them aren't even perverts.

I've never got it. New things? Have they never heard of old things? Old, reliable things. Things you can predict the outcome of and already know you don't hate doing? And if these people like trying new things so much, why do they never give shutting up a go? Personally I've always been a big fan of a comfort zone, yet that phrase is pretty much exclusively used to describe something you need to leave as quickly as possible. Why is something with such a cosy-sounding name being treated like an on-fire hotel? Come on. A whole zone, just for me to feel comfort in? Yes, please, pop it next to the quiet carriage.

Obviously I understand getting out of your comfort zone is how you progress. I get that you need purpose and you can't sit still for ever without your life fading into oblivious nothing, or ending up on a Channel 5 documentary called *Two Tonne Tony*. What I also know is that once you leave your comfort zone, all you're really doing is slowly building a new comfort zone somewhere else. Some comedians are criticised for not leaving their 'comfort zone' to try something more ambitious and genre-bending, as though the act of doing stand-up comedy isn't already a daunting, bucket-list cliché itself. In fact, I know it is, because it appears on Bored Panda's list of Top 10 Spontaneous Things to Do. But even stand-up comedy becomes a comfort zone eventually. Everything does, if you do it enough. Three years into doing it myself, I came off-stage at the Comedy Store in Manchester to another comic asking me how it had gone, and without stopping to consider the answer, I said, 'Boring.' Boring! I had found the *stand-up comedy* performance I had done to an *audience* of *hundreds* to be tedious. It had gone well. The crowd enjoyed it. It was just . . . unexceptional. Regular. I had played that venue, done that material, countless times before. Boooring.

Often it's the feeling of having completed the daunting act that appeals, rather than the act itself. Having taken a big risk and not ending up dead, or mangled. Why is it that basically every good emotion comes off the back of pushing through a bad one? Why must every reward only be worthwhile if we work for it? Can't there be a couple of good feelings for free? Every high requires enormous effort. Or at the very least has infuriating consequences, like hangovers or Type 2 diabetes.

I don't find stand-up boring any more. Every professional rut has been solved by new material. Coming up with it, making it work, building something from nothing. It's starting over. You couldn't pay me to do my first-ever gig again, the mountain is too big to climb, but my God I'd kill for the buzz of having *just* done it. I guess I love trying new things, me.

The problem I've found is, if you spend too much time in one comfort zone, the other ones you built begin to shrink, and you dread ever taking that first step back towards them. Do you know that feeling when you're meeting a group at a pub and you don't know where they're sat, so you have to awkwardly wander around until you spot one of them, then ask a bunch of people with three-quarters-full pints if anyone wants a drink, before scuttling off to the bar alone, only to return to the table to try and squeeze your way into a pre-existing conversation? That's how I feel all the time about everything. It's not a big deal, it's a slight inconvenience, a momentary obstacle to an eventual good time, that somehow acts as a deterrent for me to ever bother doing anything.

There's a popular word for that feeling these days, which I'm remiss to use, so if you in no way relate to that scenario, then you probably don't have 'it'. But for me, I stand frozen outside that metaphorical and literal pub every time, staring at the door, wondering what my life will be like if I don't go in. If I go home, or switch off my phone and disappear for ever. Suddenly I'm twelve again, standing at the skatepark, watching it all happen around me. That's how I know I have to push through. I can't stand at the top of the halfpipe holding my skateboard my whole life. I have to drop in. Everything's easier after the first time.

Nowhere is this sentiment more true than with sex. Is there anything in the world with a more marked improvement between go number one and go number two than sexual intercourse? And without even getting any coaching. Just an incredible amount of new-found knowledge. So *that's* how that works! Oh, *that's* what that feels like! Well, *that's* further back than I expected! It's akin to the feeling of striking oil, or discovering America. You might not be an expert, but you're aeons away from the absolute beginner you were ninety seconds ago. Suddenly all those training videos you watched actually make logistical sense. It's the pinnacle of 'learn-by-doing', and frankly, the ultimate 'comfort zone'.

Good old sexual intercourse. Come to think of it, is there any kind of intercourse other than sexual? Why do we keep clarifying our intercourse? No one has ever said the word 'intercourse' and made you think of anything other than banging. Technically it refers to any interaction between people, but if someone told you they'd had pleasant 'intercourse' with the postman earlier you'd think they were a filthy slag.

Despite the appeal, it's still a daunting prospect to have sex for the first time, particularly for a late bloomer obsessed with not being embarrassed who had his pants pulled down at school. It's been levelled at me in various comedy roast formats that I look like a Mormon, so it won't come as a surprise to learn I also used to live like one, harnessing a historic relationship with sex governed by fear and shame. And, to be fair, most of my best work was missionary.

I managed to keep my trepidation a secret by very cleverly talking about nothing other than boners, boobs and cum for several years, like all the other lads my age, though I learned a difficult lesson about shortening that to 'BBC'. But in spite of myself, my teen years were not without opportunity. On more than one occasion (see: two occasions), I found myself mid-make-out marathon, actively moving another's hand off the crotch of my jeans, despite clear evidence that I wanted it there. It felt in the moment like I could play it off as a sort of finger-wagging 'oh, how naughty' flirtation, pretending I was such a master of the craft I wanted to continue the foreplay for ever, to really make it worthwhile. But as the immortal words 'Do you not want to?' entered my ears, followed by the urgent squeak of 'Not really' exiting my mouth, I realised I was the first teenage boy in history to be a prick-tease to himself.

Naturally, given my previous form, I didn't *tell* anyone about this. I had to save face, even if that face was bright red and now stained with watermelon lip gloss. I knew that social cachet in your teenage years was mostly built on lies about sexual conquests and saying the word 'pussy' as many times as possible. So if the information was out there that I had spent the night in the same bed as a girl, why would I fill anyone in the morning after, when I had failed to do exactly that the night before? For me, it was always a tap of the nose and a cheeky wink. A gentleman never tells (when he is the victim of his own extremely embarrassing tale). Sorry, but some things are private (specifically my own privates, which I kept to myself). Mum's the word (I typed into my phone contacts as I called her to come and pick me up, as per). That is one of the earliest life lessons I ever learned: anyone claiming to be 'keeping their cards close to their chest' doesn't have any cards. No one has ever kept good news a secret.

Important to say, for balance, I didn't always operate with such 1950s-style class and decorum in terms of my braggadocio. This is the same guy who faked injuries to get out of games and pretended to have already done drugs to get out of . . . doing drugs. By this point I was already a fully paid-up member of the 'Definitely Not a Virgin' club, which, in hindsight, was quite a counterproductive name in terms of how it made people think of you. But with no prior girlfriends to fake-notch on my fake-bedpost, my fabrication had to be creative.

Typically this manifests in the all-time classic claim that 'she goes to a different school', which I fear, sadly, has been killed by the invention of social media. At one time, that claim was thrown out as a nameless hypothetical, trading on the exoticism of a *different* school, which may as well be a different planet. 'You mean, somewhere other than this here brick and mortar?' the other boys would ask, like Sumerians asking Adam to describe Eden. 'Yes,' would come the response, from a confident boy now staring off into the distance like a French explorer. 'A new world, where you call the teachers by their first name and wearing a tie is optional. Where there's no such thing as detention and the dinner bell is a wind-chime. Where hope runs free . . . and the girls are loose. That one's crucial.'

Sure, it raised questions of how and where you met, and how it could be possible that a virgin who's had zero luck with girls he's known for years and sees every day could leverage a chance encounter with a stranger into an instant one-night stand despite having no experience or expertise. But your peers would be more fascinated in your tales of the other side, of what paths you must've traversed to get there, of what wonders may one day await them.

These days, the ability to find out every bit of information about everyone and everything on the internet in twelve seconds has put that lie, ironically, to bed. You'd have to pick a specific person to lie about getting off with, knowing your friends also have the ability to communicate directly with said suspect to find out the truth in humiliating, screenshot-table fashion. Things were marginally more primitive in my day, but the early trappings of MySpace coupled with an incestuous small-town environment meant this path was a real no-go.

The other option was to claim it happened on holiday, as if adolescent family holidays took place in Magaluf rather than, say, Disneyland, which, despite being one of the most popular locations for marriage proposals, is possibly the most sexless place on Earth. Even if summers weren't spent at theme parks for children, but Benidorm or Devon, family holidays are about snorkelling in a swimming pool, eating Lays on a balcony, and pissing off your brother. They are not about boning strangers.

So, through process of elimination, I cooked up my own version of this world-famous lie, and told my friend Fred that I, a fifteen-year-old boy with six pubes and a fear of his own skateboard, had successfully had intercourse (sexual), with a girl from 'athletics club', called Natalie. Where I felt this tale had some credibility was: a) I did not know Natalie's surname, thus she could not be traced with much ease, and b) No one Fred was friends with attended athletics club, so there was no one to corroborate or contradict my story. (Another life lesson: never trust someone who's actively trying to avoid having a witness.)

Where the idea falls down is literally every other aspect of the scenario. For starters, athletics club was something I attended on Tuesday nights between the ages of thirteen and fifteen, with my brother, driven by our mum, who would wait in the tuck shop for the duration. The 'club' I refer to was a floodlit 400-metre track with some empty crowd stands, at which we were 'trained' by an eighteen-year-old saving up to go to Thailand, but felt at the time like a 35-year-old former Olympic medallist. Natalie was the only girl who attended.

It wasn't that I wanted to sleep with Natalie. I've made my fears about that sort of thing quite clear. It was more that I didn't have the imagination to think up a single other female name, when pressed with Fred's interrogative expertise of, 'Oh yeah, what's her name then?' The questions I'd have asked if I were Fred are: 'Where did this happen?' given the only option outside of the staffed and, crucially, mum-monitored tuck shop was the high-jump crash mat in the dead centre of the running track. And: 'When did it happen?' given the only gap in running was when I'd demand to skip hurdles because they 'hurt my side'. Another implausible lie, though I do now see the irony in *literally* refusing to jump over any hurdles. You can't fall at the first one if you don't do them to begin with, I guess.

Nothing about my story checked out. Was I claiming this was why I always left athletics hot and flustered? Was I suggesting *this* was the warm-down? Or is the story itself the only real stretch. It was completely preposterous, and all it would take was one look at my stature, braces, babyface and general demeanour to realise it was completely impossible that I could ever have had sex.

Thankfully, Fred let it slide. I could tell by the glint in his eye that he knew I was talking nonsense, but he opted not to call me out on it. Maybe out of generosity, or maybe he was busy thinking about the girl he'd met on the French exchange, whose name he couldn't remember, but who sounded stunning, and very promiscuous.

So stuck in my own denial was I that I once lied about how many sexual partners I'd had during a doctor's appointment. I was newly eighteen, and that number remained, in reality, zero, but when I went to check a potential lump on my testicle, my brain defaulted to its usual bluster the second I heard the question, and I said . . . fourteen. *Fourteen*. He looked the exact same way every doctor does when you tell them you only drink two units of alcohol a week. I watched on as he wrote something down in his notes that was definitely not the shape of a one and a four. It was when he then asked if some student doctors could join in with the physical nut examination in order to 'learn', and I said absolutely not, before leaving his office to go and have a panic attack in the toilets, that he must've been really sold on my shagging credentials. 'Wow,' he probably thought. 'Now this is a guy who *fucks*.'

It's easy to understand now how dark it was to lie about all this sort of stuff, particularly at a young age. But virginity was spoken about in such a baffling fashion. For girls, it was seen as a purity that must be protected until the circumstances are perfect, certainly in books and on TV. Female friends would rally against this, encouraging each other to stop being 'frigid' and get on with it, the more experienced assuring the others it's not all that important, a sentiment the boys would echo. That is, until a girl actually did lose it, at which point she'd become a 'slag', and must be publicly sneered at, while privately DM'd. For boys, you're pressured into getting rid of your virginity as quickly as possible, like a murder weapon, although it's perfectly permissible to tell everyone exactly where you disposed of it.

One of the most painful things about being a teenager is how inauthentically you have to live, partly because it's all a big game of fitting in, but mainly because you don't have any idea how to be authentic yet. It's so difficult to know what's real about yourself when you're young. It baffles me that I spent so much of my teens copying whichever group I was hanging around with, and now I do a job that rewards uniqueness. In some ways, that's just being a frightened kid, but it's probably not helped by a school system built on creating all-rounders for a world that rewards specialists.

If I were really honest with my friends at school, they'd have seen there was something I specialised in already. No, it was not 'crushing pussy' as I, and they, claimed. On the contrary, I was a sensitive, hopeless romantic, consumed by the sleepless angst of unrequited yearning, heavy with the weight of my own desire. I was a pussy. And it was crushing. So much of my adolescence was spent writing poems and lyrics for and about girls I liked, who didn't like me back.

I understand this is about as original as making a mix CD, which I of course also did, but just because something is unoriginal, does it make it any less valid? Was Michelangelo the first person to paint a ceiling? And perhaps my own attempts were elevated by the fact I also learned basic Photoshop skills in order to make cover art for such mix CDs, as well as a track-listing to slot into the back of them. I was my own little HMV (Hopeless Miserable Virgin).

During my cloying affection for one poor subject, who I held in my desires like a rabbit in the vice-tight grip of Lenny from *Of Mice and Men*, I even bought us tickets to see one of the mix CD's musicians, which, to age us, was Kate Nash. True to everything that has ever happened in my life, in the interim between booking said tickets and actually going to said concert, said subject got herself a boyfriend. How would it play out, I wondered? Would he be so threatened by such an old-fashioned romantic he'd ask to take my place at the gig? Maybe he'd even demand she not attend at all? No. Of course not. He drove us to the train station himself and saw us off with a smile.

Slightly more unique is the time I sent a single rose on Valentine's Day to a girl I had never actually met, and who had likely never heard of me until reading my name on the card. There used to be something quite romantic about the idea of having a 'secret admirer', back when it was the culmination of stolen glances in the office. A cheeky Valentine was a way to test the water for breaking that sexual tension at the next 'away day'. There's something more sinister about a secret admirer who is a local stranger that has somehow found your address and then not even bothered to keep themselves a secret. At best that's a bit too 'cat burglar' to be romantic. At worst it's full 'Zodiac Killer'.

Sometimes I wonder if I was even being authentic in my heartache. Sure, I stood out from the crowd of walking boners that was my friendship group, who all but humped any hand that happened to curl itself into a circle. But there was someone else on the scene inspiring my imitation. His name was Seth Cohen, a fictional high school kid in American TV show *The O.C.* You see, Seth (played by a 25-year-old Adam Brody) was a seventeen-year-old outcast, considered weird for liking comic-book superheroes (the most popular characters in the history of entertainment), and not being a sports-playing jock (despite having a six-pack and being objectively gorgeous). However, he eventually won the affection of his obsession, Summer Roberts, through a series of romantic gestures and Hail Marys, as she realised the boy who'd been privately drawing pictures of her since he was seven probably was, in fact, the one. It's a tale as old as time. Creepy loner harasses popular stunner until they finally relent. I'm wiping tears from my eyes just thinking about it, although it could be the pepper spray.

At this point in my life, I was fully trying to be Seth. I was dressing like him (sweater-vests over shirts), talking like him (incorrectly using the word 'percolate') and even watching things he had watched in the show despite not liking them (*Hellboy*, VH1). I have always had an extremely obsessive nature, where something will completely consume me for a brief burst of time and become my entire identity, before I abandon it for ever, finding it extremely embarrassing in hindsight (see also: *Smash Hits* magazine, the Bedingfields, collecting small ornamental skulls). The problems with my attempts at full Sethification were that I did not have the facial structure, dazzling charm or strapping athleticism of a Hollywood actor in his mid-twenties. Nor did I have the award-winning writing team of a 'will-they, won't-they?' American teen drama. What I had was poems, personalised CDs, regular nosebleeds and two tickets to Kate Nash. And that's not enough. If anything, it's way, way too much.

Incredibly, I thought this side of me was one I was keeping under wraps. But it turns out if you wear your heart on your sleeve, people will see it. Especially if you're in a sweater-vest. In Sixth Form I edited the school magazine (obviously), and the month in which I ran for Head Boy (obviously), another student did a double-page spread of all the candidates' strengths and weaknesses in the form of Pokémon cards (obviously). Typically those strengths would be things like 'has some good ideas for restructuring the common room kitchenette' and weaknesses along the lines of 'maybe slightly too distracted playing county rugby to be a good leader'. Can you imagine the depths to which my jaw dropped when I saw that my own weaknesses section simply said 'owner of an achy breaky heart'?

How did he know? What is it about teenagers that means they can see you for who you are no matter what kind of masking you think you may be doing? How do they possess both the analytical HUD vision of the Terminator and the acerbic, barbed word economy of A. A. Gill? And why must they use them both for evil?

I couldn't argue though. It reminded me of being called 'weird' while walking to primary school one morning, for complaining to Fred, 'I don't have anyone to fancy at the moment.' What an unnatural, overly calculated way to try and experience love. It wasn't even companionship I wanted. It was the longing itself. I didn't want anyone to be my girl-friend; I wanted to wish someone would be. In some ways this isn't different to the modern app-based dating process. A list of candidates to assess, before choosing a frontrunner to fawn over, like Simon Cowell standing over a desk of head-shots. I was so full of urges and feelings I didn't understand as a child that I desperately wanted somewhere to put them. The sort of pent-up adolescent angst that could only be solved with regular exercise, perhaps somewhere like athletics club.

Flashback to Valentine's Day 1998, when I, at seven years old, did a felt-tip drawing of myself standing with coy pigeon toes and holding a heart-shaped balloon, and wrote a love letter on the back of it and anonymously placed it in the tray of the girl I fancied. In primary school, everyone had their own tray. You got given a tray and a peg. If you lost some-thing, there were only two places it could be. What a simple time that was, back when our whole world could fit in a little plastic drawer, and a peg was part of your day-to-day, rather than something people ask for on special occasions. I still remember the hot shame of seeing Caitlin Cox and her friends gather around her handmade Valentine in the playground, trying to identify the boy in the drawing, like detectives cross-referencing a police sketch. I wasn't hard to find: I had drawn myself with embarrassed rosy cheeks.

It may shock you to learn that she, along with one other

girl mentioned in this chapter, did turn out to be eventual kissing partners for your boy Penguin. Sure, several years later, but all thanks to a little something known as 'laying the groundwork'. Foreplay for ever. One of the remaining two has since come out as gay, and the other one moved all the way to Australia, which I'm assured is a decision that has nothing to do with me. Or so she said when I tracked her down on Instagram to ask.

There's something extremely precocious about being a teenage boy who was already looking for love, rather than meaningless sex. And by precocious I mean I was the only sixteen-year-old lad with the exact same motivations as Carrie Bradshaw. But the real emotional mangle was well after adolescence, in the university Christmas breaks, when we'd all return to our small close-knit town, eager to show off our new selves, but forced to reminisce about our old ones. The exoticism of a different school when you're a teenager is squashed on day one of university, where, unless you go to Oxbridge, you're exposed to all sorts of people, from those who call lunch 'dinner', to those who call tea 'supper'. It's a complete enlightenment. And so, the window to the rest of the world that you pressed yourself up against, wondering what someday might be, becomes a window to the past that you stare through more wistfully, wondering what might've been. At university you broaden your horizons, try those 'new things' people bang on about, find a new style, speak in a new cadence, maybe even grow into your awkward face. And while you enjoy that for what it is, at least some of that time is spent wishing everyone from before could see you now. Who you've become. Who you always wanted to be. Your new hairstyle. The lot.

This is why the most emotionally, romantically and sexually

charged night in the calendar is Christmas Eve. From the ages of about eighteen to twenty-four, it was the custom in my town to go to the pub on Christmas Eve, as that was where literally everyone you'd ever come into contact with would be, now more mature, more open-minded, and with more stubble. It never descends into a full night out. We hold no space for 'Christmas clubbers'. Christmas Eve is a night for sentimentality. It's for *conversations* over *pints*, not VK strawpedos to Katy Perry's 'Cozy Little Christmas'. The night starts with your own friendship group, picking up the same running jokes and memories, interspersed between reminders of what course you each do, before every squeeze to the bar or toilet sees you absorbed by a different group of lesser friends, warm with the welcome of Yuletide, keen to embrace you as their own, like an overly earnest advert for Samaritans, or Iceland.

As the night goes on, however, the real Christmas magic can begin, as everyone works their way through various ex-flames, to laugh about how awkward they used to be, so as to put distance between that loser back then and the suave lothario they've learned to be at Nottingham Trent. It's all a play to shift the power balances of unrequited longing from yesteryear. To say: we're not in double science any more, honey, I'm a new man! To reframe the memories, by reimagining them with the you from right now, instead of the actual you from back then. Eventually conversation turns to the relationship itself, and the weakest participant, trapped in the crosshairs, utters the infamous, 'Why were we never a thing?' subconsciously admitting what you already know to be true: that you've become ever so slightly fitter, or at least a bit less humiliating to be seen with.

Of course, this never manifests into anything bigger than the sum of its parts. It's simple nostalgia. At most, this is followed by a cheeky 'Merry Christmas' text the next morning, saying how nice it was to catch up and how you must go for a drink that'll never happen. Possibly even a Christmas Eve kiss, if you've been completely Love Actualised into believing in fairy tales that particular year. But never, ever more than that. It's Christmas Eve for crying out loud! Show some respect to our lord and saviour, Richard Curtis. You're on the tightrope walk of hypotheticals. Actually following through with anything is to slip to your death.

I am aware we're a nation divided. Some people can't believe anyone goes out on Christmas Eve. They're shocked at this flagrant disregard for the sanctity of family and tradition. 'How can you hang your stocking drunk?' they say. 'Don't you want to be in your pyjamas watching *Elf* with a hot chocolate?' 'How will you open your special "early" present if you're down The Old Cock Inn?' There are a couple of explanations for these people. In some cases, they live beyond walking distance to the local, and thus the impracticality of the whole thing makes it more hassle than it's worth. In others, they are infantilised little freaks who use words like 'toesies' and 'holibobs' and refuse to explore even a single second of their own thoughts for fear it might reveal they accidentally possess multitudes.

Or they didn't grow up in a small town where everyone knows each other and this is the done thing. Each to their own, I say.

Eventually, of course, you move on. You make way for a new generation of lovers and dreamers. Your parents move away from that hometown. Your friends start to have children of their own. This is a good thing. Nostalgia can only take you so far. In the seventeenth century, when the word was first coined, 'nostalgia' was considered a psychological disorder and treated as a disease, with sufferers said to be 'manic with longing'. The reason anyone cared was that it was affecting soldiers and their ability to, well, soldier, as they 'longed' 'manically' for the past in which they, oh, I don't know . . . maybe, weren't at war? Some countries treated it with leeches to the stomach; others made it punishable by death. Some simply sent soldiers home, to return to that for which they yearned. The word itself comes from the Greek *nostos*, or homecoming, and *algos*, or pain, which does do quite a good job of summing up my Christmas Eve theory, although these days there's so much more to nostalgia than pain. Maybe it made sense to think everyone who felt nostalgic in the seventeenth century was clinically insane, given how shit the early seventeenth century was. Why would you possibly long for that, you idiot? People hit a hoop with a stick for fun and died of diarrhoea. It was rubbish.

Now, nostalgia refers to everything from pining for the butterflies you felt after your first kiss, to remembering the old Nickelodeon jingle. I don't think it's mad to ruminate about the past when it informs so much of the present. Christmas Eve wasn't so much about reliving the pain of teenage heartbreak as it was re-contextualising it as a necessary part of the journey. Couple that with a smidge of rewriting history, for your own bit of harmless delusional closure, and you've turned that trauma chapter into a new 'comfort zone' for yourself. A Christmas miracle.

Everything is easier after the first time. But nothing's as *exciting* as the first time, is it? I don't feel nostalgic for any of those past flames any more, and certainly not for any of my adolescent sexual fear. I don't really feel nostalgic for anything. Someday I'm sure I'll yearn for the past again. I'll read the poems I wrote that at one time represented me, then embarrassed me, then explained me, and I'll wonder who they were even about, and what it was like to feel that way. And one day, my penis won't work, and I'll think back to the times I literally hid erections from willing consumers of them because I was shy, and I'll be absolutely furious. But right now I'm not fussed about any of that. I'm just trying to get some new material.

Shrinking Violet

I completed therapy after four sessions. Do you have any idea how fast that is? People have therapy for years, sometimes their whole lives. Not me. A swift four weeks. In and out. Summer camp. It's the equivalent of someone, mid-argument, telling you to 'chill out', and then you actually doing it, immediately, for ever. But that's just me, I guess. I'm built different.

Is it definitely healthy to see my record therapy time as an achievement, thereby suggesting I always viewed mental health as a competition? Probably not. But right now the only weight on my shoulders is my gold therapy medal, so who cares?

It was May 2023 and I had been on tour for the past four months, which was due to end with my biggest solo show to date at the Hackney Empire, a venue I had wanted to play since before I had performed at my very first pub basement fourteen years earlier. For the first time since the tour started, I had an entire free week in advance of it. Perfect, I thought. I can go and do some real-life things and come to it completely refreshed, like a bride-to-be pampering before her wedding, except I was charging entry to my big day. I mentally limbered up for my 'holiday', dusting off tennis rackets and golf clubs, googling local spas, checking cinema listings, ordering classic novels. Things that would help me become zen, things that would give me enough perspective not to panic, things I hadn't had time to do all year.

When the week rolled around, however, I found myself completely paralysed. All day I'd sit, pinned to my minimalist Danish armchair, much to the displeasure of the cat, whose incredibly expensive spot it usually is. Not really doing anything. Mindlessly browsing things on my laptop, taking nothing in. An hour would go by and I'd think, I really ought to get up and do something. But I wouldn't. I'd just sit there. Doing nothing. Another hour. 'Wow, I'm really wasting the day,' I'd say to myself. 'Maybe now would be a good time to sort out—' Nope. More sitting. More clicking. More staring.

Maybe you've had the experience of getting so engrossed in your work or a video game that the room has got dark without you noticing. Usually this is broken up by a mum, preferably your own, breezing in to say, 'Shall we have some lights on?' But not this time. There's no mum to fix everything now. I've let the day get dark on me, too absorbed in nothing to even notice. Suddenly it's bedtime, and I traipse upstairs, telling myself that was what my brain needed, to switch off entirely, pleading with myself not to feel guilty, bargaining that there's another chance tomorrow. By 3 p.m. the next day I've changed my to-do list to say 'sit in chair' in a desperate bid to cheat-code my own sense of accomplishment.

The show is on Friday. On Thursday I realise I've spent four days in the same browser cycle: emails – Twitter – YouTube – *Guardian Culture* – other email account – Twitter – *Telegraph* crosswords – emails – pick up phone to look at Instagram – TikTok – emails on phone – Twitter on phone (in Safari because I deleted the app so I can't look at it) – Instagram – back to laptop in case anyone's emailed me there – Twitter (now in

Safari on laptop because I've blocked it on Google Chrome so I can't look at it) – YouTube – BBC homepage – emails – Carhartt sale – YouTube – Tumblr account of my mad conspiracy theorist stalker who thinks I'm part of an elitist political plot – Twitter (Safari) – emails – Instagram on laptop.

When you're looking at Instagram in a browser window on your laptop, you know you've fully lost your mind. When you find your eyes drifting from the laptop Instagram to look at the same Instagram post on your phone, you need to be put down. I don't remember blinking for that entire forty-eight hours, but I must've done. Then again, everything was out of focus by that point, so maybe not.

Suddenly my browsing turned to something new. Google. Everything was still happening on autopilot, so I was also a spectator, excited to see what new world awaited. We can't get ahead of ourselves here; sometimes it's a misdirect and I don't really need to google anything, my fingers have simply decided to take the scenic route to YouTube. Or I'm looking up my own name again, only to find misspelt articles about hamstring injuries at Chelsea. But not this time. I found myself staring at a website I'd never seen before, typing in my postcode, scrolling through a list of names and photos. Stephen, London Bridge, Qualified Psychotherapist. Jeanette, Bromley-by-Bow, PhD in Psychology. These were therapists. I was looking at therapists. How did I get here? Did I doomscroll so much it was the only website I hadn't been on yet? Or had I just subconsciously staged my own intervention?

The problem with needing to get therapy because you don't like anything and you're too judgemental is how difficult that makes it to select a therapist. I scrolled through those mental health professionals like I was on Tinder. Not her, I went to a better uni than that. Not him, he's an adult man with blond hair. No chance, she clearly got that photo done at Snappy Snaps. He looks too much like Super Hans. Eventually though, I developed an astute scientific method with which to narrow it down: pick the guy who has the most qualifications.

Why did I think that mattered? What's the point in being more qualified than you need to be? So long as he's legally allowed to be a practitioner, surely that's enough. When you get in a taxi, you simply expect they've passed their driving test, you don't care if they're ordained and have a licence to teach scuba diving. Would you respect someone more if they had 200 GCSEs? Obviously not, you'd respect them far, far less. But this was the metric on which I made my choice. The most qualified and, more importantly, the most expensive. Which I assumed meant he was the best, because I'm pathetic.

I sent him an email and he replied alarmingly promptly (which suddenly explained how he'd had so much time to get so many certificates) suggesting a quick phone call to establish what I was looking for to see if he could help. I toyed with saying I wanted to enrol in the Open University and was keen to know if he'd recommend it, but I stuck to the therapy and asked if the call would be free. He said yes, outside of your service provider costs, which was the sort of droll comeback he probably learned on a comedy course, knowing him. I ignored the fact he missed an opportunity to say, 'Always ask the bill payer's permission,' and dialled his number. 'What is it you're struggling with?' he said, in that way-too-soft therapist cadence that makes you feel sick. And six. I paused for thought, which they love. 'I can't remember how to do things.'

He paused back, which I hated. 'What do you . . . mean by

that?' he offered, as soft as a cock on the antidepressants I hoped he'd give me.

'I . . . I don't think I know how to enjoy things any more.'

The world is full of people claiming to be happy. Whether they're lying to everyone via carefully curated Instagram carousels, or deluding themselves that one day a spouse or job might get better. They think if you hide the sadness from the world, eventually it will disappear. And no group is worse for this than the New Age positivity nutters. You know the sort, they bang on about 'energy' and 'love' in their preachy voices that are either too high or too slow, and they're weirdly into sparkling water. Their kryptonite is negative thoughts. If you slag something off in their presence, they put their fingers in their ears like they're trying to avoid a spoiler, and say something about not putting that into the universe, as if negative thoughts are non-recyclable and the universe is the green bin. They flat-out refuse to hear any criticism. No criticism of themselves, no criticism of others. Certainly not of overpriced crystals. And they think they're the ones who have life figured out, when in reality they're the most unhinged and dangerous freaks among us.

These are people who believe that not only is it possible, but that it's optimal to feel only happy all the time, and they pursue this with badly researched daily routines of freakishly early bedtimes and scheduled meditation. They say phrases like 'circadian rhythm' and expect us to know that's not a reggae band. They've given up alcohol and refuse to acknowledge they've replaced it with protein yoghurts. They refer to themselves as 'empaths' despite having no empathy with how fucking annoying everyone finds them. They are positivity nutters. Or, more realistically, they're pretending to be. Look in their eyes and you'll see this is not the look of a happy person. It's the plastered-on enthusiasm of a kids' TV presenter with an obvious hangover.

I'm not saying there's nothing good about their methods. Obviously I understand there are benefits to cold plunging. Apparently ice baths are great for relieving stress, particularly when you get out of them. But it's difficult to trust anything also popular with the purveyors of 'rise and grind', a business-hustle mentality pushed by pseudo-scientific 'gurus' on social media, being aggressively American over the *Dark Knight* soundtrack.

The last decade has been monumental for mainstream mental health awareness, but that's been hijacked by a whole sub-section of society who are only able to talk about mental health in regard to making money. They're obsessed with maximising productivity, despite the fact they don't actually seem to do anything.

The lie they sell is that you're only in competition with yourself. The moment you stop comparing yourself to others and focus on your own goals, you'll find it much easier to succeed. Succeed, that is, in maximising profits for your business and crushing the competition. If these people are only competing with themselves, then who are they getting up earlier than? Who are they trying to get an advantage over? People have limits, and once you're at yours, you're just shifting the timeframe, not extending it. If you're constantly getting up five minutes earlier, eventually it's yesterday again and you didn't go to bed.

What they're selling is the product of your future happiness. And meal replacement drinks, of course. What they claim is the secret to that happiness is success. And yet pretty much every successful, rich, famous person ever asked has explained that it is process, not results, that actually fulfils you. That relationships are more important than money. So why do we let these gurus and grifters tell us they know best? Surely if they were as rich and successful as they claim, they too would be telling us how pointless it all was?

Anyone sane knows that it's not a bad thing to experience the full range of the emotional spectrum once in a while. Yes, faking a smile can release endorphins and serotonin, elevating your mood. But how incredibly soulless is it to get your joy manually? A smile is what you do because you feel happiness. Happiness isn't what you feel because you smile. The whole thing feels like the panicked excuse of a man who's been caught cat-calling a woman. 'No, trust me, it's *good* for you! It releases chemicals. *That's* why I told you to smile. I was actually trying to help you, love. I mean *miss*.' We're two years away from being told faking an orgasm can actually release cum.

Feeling sad is good. It hurts, but it sure makes you notice when you don't any more. Is there a greater euphoria than the laugh you do at the end of a cry? When your tears are starting to run out and someone crouches in front of you to say something semi-sarcastic from beneath your bowed head. 'Still, look on the bright side, at least you don't have to pretend to like Morrissey any more!' Cue snotty laughter. Tension broken! Light through a cloud! Human connection! It's no use plastering on a smile and pretending everything's fine by blocking out negative thoughts. You can't fake it 'til you make it to happiness. Eventually something's got to give. There's only so much joviality you can force on your own brain until eventually you snap and strangle a lollipop lady, or start doing TikTok dances with your family. You can only be Ned Flanders for so long before you're turning to Homer and screaming: 'BREATHE THROUGH YOUR DAMN NOSE!'

A far more reasonable claim for mental health is exercise. Rather than training your cheek muscles all day with fake grins, why not train a whole bunch of muscles, and provide yourself an outlet for all that negative energy? Maybe you're a 35-year-old dad in East London, in which case you're probably going to want to get back into five-a-side football on a week-night. And yes, you can cycle there, Rufus. But best of luck finding nine friends. Or maybe you're a young woman, desperate to escape the toxic poison of everything told to you by a magazine, TV programme or older relative until you were six-teen? Time to lift some weights and get swole. Girlboss, gaslight, Grenade bars. Or perhaps you dislike the fake smilers so much, you want to go the other way and deny yourself joy altogether, instead choosing constant rage, frustration and anguish? Easy. Golf.

The most accessible, of course, is running. Unfortunately my brain won't let me continue forward motion unless I'm being chased, or a train door is beeping, both of which can be difficult to organise. So instead, I favour the gym. For a long time, I was anti the whole place, choosing to believe I wasn't made for it. That I am a thinker, a philosopher, and words are my weights. But then I realised sentences like that are the sort that get you beaten up, so I should probably get some muscles in case.

For months I had listened to friends of mine tell me how good the gym was for mental health, which strikes me as counterproductive. 'Oh yes, I feel a bit down about myself today, why don't I go to the place where everyone's sexy and I'm bad at everything?' Let me tell you what's not great for self-esteem: having to ask a bigger boy to get the lid off your protein powder for you. And yet, it works. To watch yourself improve in real time, to not have your progression be in someone else's hands. To actually only be in competition with yourself, which is great, because you always win. But kind of bad, given you also always lose. Frankly, in the gym, I'm the only one I'm *willing* to compete with. I'm not getting anywhere near a podium against the Under Armour freaks in that place. Perhaps that's the secret? Pick opponents that are far better than you. It's much easier to stop comparing yourself to others if they're uncatchable. It's easy not to be jealous of Bob Mortimer when I'd rather watch him as well.

You do have to wonder, though, is it the working-out itself that's good for your mind, or is it the being sexy? Sure, you may go to the gym for the endorphins and dopamine and the sense of progress, but the by-product of all that is that your body becomes a lot more Chris Pratt in *Avengers* and a lot less Chris Pratt in *Parks and Recreation*. Bits shrink, other bits grow, everything gets tighter or harder. These are sex words. You get sexier. And therein lies your mental health. In the interests of self-preservation, I do acknowledge the fact all body shapes can be sexy. What the gym turns you into, however, has been held up as the archetypal *sexy* body for centuries. It rests on the *Love Island* daybeds, fills skin-tight superhero suits on cinema screens and was toiled over by ancient sculptors. What could've been better for David's mental health than watching Michelangelo carve out his six-pack? And what could've been worse than seeing how little clay he picked up when it was time to do the penis. Sorry, Davey. There's no machine for that in a Fitness First.

That's not to say the gym is a guaranteed confidence builder. You can fail to lift a weight you previously nailed with ease. You can catch a glimpse of yourself at the wrong angle in one of a thousand mirrors. You can get stuck for forty minutes in that weird tube you enter through and have to bang on the glass like a forgotten *Take Me Out* contestant. Or, like me, you can be forced to do a demonstration to a full class of schoolchildren on one of the most sexual pieces of equipment ever created.

One unassuming Wednesday, in the pursuit of that sweet exercise buzz, I found myself in my local gym working even harder than normal. No more half measures, I thought. Every blog, men's health article and fitfluencer says the only way to progress in the gym is to work out until failure, performing reps until you can rep no more. So that's what I did, and it was exhausting. Buoyed but sweaty, and facing a ten-minute walk home, I decided to take a short rest on one of the vacant leg machines to catch my breath, closing my eyes and leaning back on the cushioned seat, turning up the volume in my noise-cancelling AirPods. I took a deep breath, when suddenly, I felt a hand on my shoulder. Probably someone wanting to use the machine, and fair enough, this is not my sofa. I opened my eyes ready to apologise and vacate, when I saw that in front of me stood twenty bored and furious-looking fourteen-year-olds. I'd wager there's few locations in which opening your eyes to see more despondent teenagers than you could legally fit in an elevator is a good thing, but on a leg machine at the gym, in shorts, has to be one of the worst, just losing out to a courtroom defendant's table, or a comedy gig.

'This is the hip abductor,' came a voice from behind me. I looked up to see it belonged to the uniformed (gym) man behind me, chaperone for the uniformed (school) gaggle of S Club Juniors in front of me. 'This kind gentleman is going to show us how to use it.'

Has the phrase 'this kind gentleman' ever been used to do

anything other than con some poor moron into doing something humiliating? 'I'm now going to juggle swords, and this kind gentleman is going to be my assistant' – cue a man in Covent Garden accepting his fate as a future amputee, purely to appease the street performer's pseudo-politeness. That's me. I'm the amputee. God, I'd have killed to not have legs for five minutes.

The hip abductor is that machine where two pads rest on your inner thighs, pushing your legs outwards, into a sort of splayed position. I don't have the exact measurements, but a midwife would've checked how dilated I was on pure instinct. The exercise is to squeeze your legs inwards, against the weight of the machine, until your thighs are close to touching. This trains you to stop manspreading, and strengthens your inner thighs so you can crouch for longer when lining up putts. Most gyms have these machines facing the wall due to how intimate and sexual they are, but I don't think that goes far enough. They should be in their own private booths or hidden behind modesty curtains, maybe even placed under one of those big circus tents used by exterminators. At the very least someone should be employed to hold a towel in front of you, like a mum at the beach. Under no circumstances should they be left out in the open for a child, or group of twenty children, to stumble upon.

A lot goes through your mind when you're faced with performing a seemingly lewd act to a gang of bored teens. Mainly, 'I hope the CCTV doesn't work in here,' but also, 'How can I win them round?' A couple of gags about Fortnite or Charli xcx to lighten the mood while I do this pervert's hokey-cokey, perhaps? The thing is, the hip abductor is an already difficult piece of equipment to use, let alone when you're exhausted from a workout. I'll never know why I sat down to rest on the most sexually charged machine in the building, and I'll certainly never know why I bothered to assume the starting position when I could've let my legs dangle. But what I will know is that I gave those kids the best damn hip abductor demonstration of their lives, and I'm sure of it, because the master of ceremonies over my shoulder made a point of complimenting my 'perfect form'. Sure, I regret the eye contact I made with three of the audience during the demonstration, and yes, the PT's suggestion to give me a round of applause was met with the loudest silence of my career. But you heard the man, *perfect* form. All you've got to be is better than you were yesterday. Well, I guess I'm screwed tomorrow then.

What's great about completing therapy in four weeks is both the therapist and I think we're responsible. Him, because I arrived with a problem and left quickly without it. Me, because he just fucking sat there while I said a load of shit out loud and worked it all out myself. After calling him to say I didn't know how to have fun any more, I half expected to turn up to our first session to see a ping-pong table and a bubble machine, but instead he opted for the more traditional approach of making me talk for four hours and four hundred non-tax-deductible pounds. I can claim stage clothes and stationery as a business expense, because apparently I couldn't do my job without them. But not therapy. That's apparently not 'necessary'. I could easily go on tour without a pen; I'd find it quite difficult if I had killed myself.

It's easy for me to be this flippant about therapy having never actually experienced clinical depression. I've been in situations where I've felt others would find it easier if I wasn't around, but I never seriously thought about sending myself to the grave, more like the Amalfi Coast. And sure, I've said I'm going to kill myself when a train is cancelled, but I've never actually had the urge to follow through with it. Particularly considering how much harder it is to throw yourself in front of a rail replacement bus. The main source of any genuine suicidal thoughts I've had are out of pure spite. Every now and then I do consider killing myself, but not because of any real anguish. I would do it for no other reason than to make someone who has been mean to me feel bad. Oh, you're going to overreact and tell me off over something minor? Trump card. I'm dead and it's your fault. Now who feels bad? Oh, you want to give me a middling write-up in a broadsheet newspaper? Bang. I'm dead now, and I've name-checked you in the suicide note. 'Lacked a coherent message', did I? How's this for a coherent message: you're a murderer. Suddenly we all remember the 'Be Kind' campaign and my death has changed reviewing for ever. Or, more realistically, three months, before everyone reverts back to their usual approach.

It's the ultimate revenge killing, except instead of assassinating my enemy, giving them sweet release, I murder their spirit and burden them with a lifetime of guilt. It's the toxic progression of a petulant child who didn't get their way and immediately packed a bag to leave home. So if years from now you hear somewhere that comedian Rhys James has killed himself, there's no need to bother with the age-old 'I guess you just never know what someone's going through' rhetoric. You'll know exactly what happened. Someone tutted when I accidentally cut in front of them in a queue, or got angry at me for leaving a dirty plate out on the side, and I saw an opportunity. Something to bear in mind when you're leaving your precious little Amazon reviews about this book.

Thankfully, we've made some genuine progress in the last

few years. It wasn't that long ago that the standard response to a man admitting they were struggling was a slap on the back and the phrase 'Don't be such a baby'. People these days are much more aware of anxiety, depression and the rest of the ragtag bunch, thanks in no small part to the term 'men's mental health', which is like mental health, but more important because it affects the most well-paid people in the world. It's so telling of insecure male consumer patterns that it has to be branded the same way other typically emasculating things are, like moisturiser and shampoo. This isn't Dove. It's Dove *For Men*. This isn't mental health. It's *men's* mental health. I'm surprised they don't call it 'Manxiety', or 'Definitely Not Gay-DHD'.

But while therapy can obviously be extremely helpful, there's a glaring logical flaw in the system. Therapy is voluntary. Anyone 'together' enough to bother taking themselves to any form of counselling is self-aware enough to not actually need it, and anyone who refuses to get therapy obviously needs it so, *so* much. Those who get therapy merely *want* therapy, if only for the chance to talk about themselves for an hour without having to pause to advertise Hello Fresh. While many of those who don't get therapy could *really* do with it. The people who think it's all a bit soft. Who push their emotions down in the moment and let them out onto one unsuspecting retail worker. Who die 'suddenly' of a heart attack at fifty-two, having had a stress twitch since they were nine. Older blokes who, when you ask if they 'want to talk', say: 'No, it's OK, I'll just have a cigarette and a stare out of the window, I'll be right as rain.'

This is why we need a second type of therapy. A stealth version, to secretly 'therapise' those who would never knowingly accept the real thing for fear of seeming weak. The people for whom branding hasn't worked, who still don't moisturise regardless of the bulldog on the bottle.

All we need to do is take the services people frequently come into contact with, secretly train the staff in counselling, and have them subtly drop their new knowledge into day-to-day conversations. Hotel receptionists should respond to: 'Hi, I'm just checking in,' with, 'No, *I'm* just checking in. How are you?' Waiters should say: 'Is everything OK with your meal?' And when you awkwardly nod with a mouth full of tagliatelle, they follow up with, 'How about your relationship with your father?' Taxi drivers asking, 'Where to?' should be prepared to follow an answer of 'Airport' with, 'You know you can't take a holiday from yourself?' This would solve the therapy problem for ever, so long as no one ever found out. With real therapy and secret therapy, the cross-section of society now receiving help would be literally everyone. Everyone except me, as I'd be the only one who knew about it. But I'm fine, because I already completed it in just four weeks.

It wouldn't even be difficult for our stealth therapists to slide in subtle diagnoses, by comparing whatever behaviours the unsuspecting 'patient' is describing as being like their neurodivergent brother, or reminding them of their depressed aunt. And this wouldn't even stick out as obtuse, given the recent spate of unsolicited mental health diagnosis currently so on trend.

There is a bit of an elephant in the room throughout this book, that much of my own behaviour could fall under a variety of neurodivergent categories, such as ADHD, autism or an anxiety disorder. I'm sure some of you have been desperate to DM me to tell me so, if you haven't already. I don't have a professional diagnosis for any of them, nor do I seek one. In some part, because I'd have to go through a whole process to get one, and if social engagements can sometimes fill me with dread, psychological examination is hardly going to fill me with glee. It's a cruelly ironic facet of anxiety that its presence in you is often the very thing that prevents you getting help for it.

But why bother getting a professional diagnosis anyway, when people on the internet will diagnose me for free? I once posted a TikTok of an observation that went as follows: 'I hate when my dishwasher hasn't finished its cycle and I'm forced to use the fork I hate the most.' Within twenty-four hours, thousands of teenagers flooded the comments with their verdict. 'Bro is autistic,' they told me. You know, how a doctor would say it. 'I'm taking a look at your test results and, OK leukaemia, go off, sis! It's giving "chemo".'

I know a few autistic people, and I think they'd find it insulting to have autism reduced to disliking a single fork. Although, bafflingly, in order to avoid algorithm filters, TikTok users don't actually use the word 'autistic', but 'acoustic', so that their posts don't get banned. After hundreds of comments calling me acoustic, I assumed they meant my audio quality was poor and I spent three weeks googling clip-on microphones. So they might've had a point. We are all on the spectrum, but some of us are counting the stars.

I get that we're all fighting our own battles, it's just that most people are doing it wrong. Sure, there may be some benefits to all this. Perhaps pinning your lips up into a smile until they stay there on their own is better than nothing. And maybe pathologising strangers on the internet isn't so bad. At the very least, it's the sign of a society taking more notice. And maybe it's an attempt to see ourselves in others, to feel less alone. Hopefully that's also the case when people comment 'this guy's ugly' and 'bro is not funny'.

One of the few things my therapist said to me in our brief relationship was that often people who experience the sort of paralysing dread and apathy I do benefit from finding a mental 'happy place' they can go to, to access a feeling that gets them over that initial hurdle of action. As a professional cynic I baulked at such a cliché platitude. But it soon dawned on me I was only doing so because when I heard the phrase 'happy place', nothing came to mind. There have been a couple of individual moments, sure, like that free warm cookie when you check into a DoubleTree hotel, or finding a tenner in the pocket of some old jeans. But nothing that felt significant enough for a go-to 'happy place'.

The one thing I knew for sure, though, was that it wasn't going to be here in this therapist's office. After a month of listening to myself bang on about how little fun I was having, I was more than ready to force my way out of my rut, if only to stop me ever having to talk about it again. In the final session, I interrupted myself to say that I was 'chatting shit' and no longer meant any of this drivel. I had presented my arguments in weeks one and two, then spent weeks three and four disputing all my previous points with logical counter-arguments to prove I was wrong. Effectively I had been paying for a spare moment to think out loud, without having to pause to advertise Grammarly.

The shrink stayed torturously silent to let me really feel my own self-loathing, although possibly was trying to come up with ways to keep my business. 'The only way to get better at having therapy is to do more of it,' I imagined him saying, suddenly pulling down a projector screen to show me a PowerPoint of his price plan. Instead, he suggested I record all my new counter-arguments to play back to myself for the next time I felt this way. Even he couldn't be arsed to listen to me any more, forfeiting my fee to let me counsel myself with my own past like a woke Ebenezer Scrooge.

As I left his office for the last time, he wished me luck, and said, 'Don't forget the happy place.' Again, it conjured little in my imagination. Lying in bed doing stupid voices to make Daphne laugh? Obviously there's nothing better, but was that really going to be the thing I'd picture to get me *out* of the house?

I spent the rest of the evening desperately searching my memory for something or somewhere I could use, and eventually more typical images started to appear. But as I focused on them, I noticed they were things I hadn't actually done, in places I hadn't actually been. They were experiences I imagined *would* be my happy place had I bothered to experience them. But I hadn't.

And so, seventeen years since the last attempt, I took it upon myself to turn them into reality. I opened up my laptop, spent around forty minutes flicking between Skyscanner and Expedia, deleting my cookies and refreshing my browser to ensure I was getting the best deal possible, and did what I should've done a long time ago. I booked a flight to Borneo. A return flight, obviously. I'm not mentally ill.

Sweet Baby James

It's a pretty common problem for people to lose their entire vocabulary the moment a doctor asks them what's wrong. I've even taken to rehearsing such conversations, humiliated by my own past failures. Maybe this is why the NHS is so overstretched? No one can efficiently explain what their issue is. The fact doctors for the most part just type what you're telling them into a special Doctor Google only they have access to shows the issue with this entire system. Couldn't they give us access to their secret medical search engine and save themselves the hassle? Doctors always hate it when you've googled symptoms yourself because apparently it's not 'reliable' and causes 'undue panic'. In reality, I think it's because that's *their* job. It's nice to be needed.

There can be fewer more vague medical complaints than, 'My side hurts.' But that's what I'd say as a nine-year-old. That's all I had the language for. I was able to clarify which side, though that much was obvious from my performative clutching, like a man in a stock photo of 'miscellaneous pain', but this diagnosis required more than a quick database search. 'My side hurts' is not useful information at all. It would be like going into cardiac arrest and complaining of a 'dodgy front'. What seems to be the problem? 'Oh, I've got a bit of a dicky body. Best of luck!'

It started during a sleepover at my friend Dan's house,

while my parents were at a James Taylor concert. Sharp shooting pains broken up by dull aches, but enough about the concert. With no more communication from me than 'ow', Dan's mum had little else to do but put me to bed and call my parents, who arrived to pick me up exactly one full concert plus encore plus train journey later. Fair enough. A few days later, when I screamed cartoonishly at the sight of blood coming out of my penis instead of the anticipated 'piss', they realised the severity of sticking around to hear 'Fire and Rain'. I've seen Fire and Rain as well, James, and they were both coming out of my knob.

And so began a series of trips to a series of doctors, escalating in importance with each visit. Referrals after referrals, urine samples after urine samples, blood tests after blood tests, with patches of numbing creams on my elbow pits as nurses complimented me on how prominent my veins were. Hardly something I'd be able to brag about to my friends, who, crucially, weren't written by Irvine Welsh. By this point, we had moved on from GPs and were making semi-regular visits to Great Ormond Street Hospital for ultrasounds, to confirm what was really going on in that elusive 'side' of mine. Effectively, I had kidney failure. My left kidney had shrivelled, and was now limping its way through about 10 per cent of the work it was supposed to be doing, leaving the other one to pick up the slack. It must've felt like Liam Gallagher.

You may be wondering why I haven't told any tales of gainful employment so far, reeling off the disastrous jobs I had before I was a stand-up comedian. Surely those are rife for embarrassment and shame, feeling like I didn't fit in? Are they so traumatic I can't even mine them for laughs years later? The reason is, I only ever had one job. Aged fifteen, I was a kitchen porter and waiter in a golf clubhouse for exactly one week before I got the sack, and rightly so. I'd spend hours making the specials board needlessly artistic to avoid having to clean any plates and, on more than one occasion, spilled peas down the back of someone I was delivering food to. In lieu of any proper table number system, like every other establishment in history, my job as waiter was to emerge from the kitchen and shout the dishes I was carrying until someone put their hand up to claim it, like some sort of lunch auction. The idea of yelling 'ham and cheese toastie' filled me with such panic, I'd often not bother, letting the food go cold before another employee would wander in and do it for me. I had one job and I did so little of it, they had me removed. So I very much empathise with my own left kidney.

During my medical visits, I was repeatedly told how normal I was by doctors and my parents alike. Lots of people have kidneys removed, and lots of people who haven't had them removed don't even realise they only have one functioning kidney anyway, they'd explain to me, in case I had any concerns I might one day have something unique about me. You literally don't even *need* two, they'd tell me, in the sort of tone a teenage girl would use to describe something as random. 'I don't even know why God gave us this extra one? It's so cringe!' But just because you don't need two of something, doesn't mean you're not going to feel weird for only having one. You technically don't need two lungs, or bollocks, or hands, or parents, but it helps. Of course, I said none of this at the time. It was all too overwhelming. I hadn't even really heard of the kidneys until I was told one of mine had failed. It must be like finding out you've got an estranged brother moments before learning he's on the sex offenders register.

I always resented the language about my condition. Kidney

failure. Failure! Unlucky, mate. Your kidney tried, but it fucked it. Sorry. 'F minus'. We all know failure is a natural part of life, and I've had my fair share, from failed podcasts (x3), to failed relationships (x2), to failed auditions (x99^{99}). But this failure wasn't part of life. It was part of *me*. I'd rather they called it kidney death. At least that has a sort of dark edge to it. But this made me feel like I literally had failure running through me. I mean, what hope did I have of possessing the requisite drive of a billionaire CEO when even my organs couldn't be arsed to do their most basic of jobs? I was constantly told 'It's what's on the inside that counts', and what was on the inside of me was defeat.

And so, out it had to come. Full Kexit. Me, the EU, ridding myself of a toxic organ that wasn't what it used to be so I could thrive, while my kidney, the UK, was studied for scientific research.

Everyone acted like something huge was going to happen, expecting me to be terrified. But I was a nine-year-old facing the prospect of two full weeks off school, universal sympathy and a cool scar. I was absolutely thrilled. If someone offers you two free tickets to an attention theme park, at which you'll be waited on hand and foot like a little prince, while all your friends have to go to their stupid little school to be taught about Tudors, you'd have only one question: 'Do I get queue jump?' 'Of course you do, pal. You're a sick kid.'

To clarify, the schools I went to were very pleasant, though maybe not as pleasant as people like to assume. In Britain, there are several different types of school. We have state schools, paid for with taxes, and Catholic schools, paid for with guilt. But one type of school in the UK receives absolutely no funding from the government whatsoever, left to stand on its own two feet and be paid for by those so hard up they often avoid paying tax themselves. These are private boarding schools. They're like normal schools, but they take place during a six-year sleepover in a manor, focusing largely on teaching posture, tutting and turning up to things extremely overdressed. They cost an absolute fortune to send your children to, and even then, money isn't always enough. Eton College, for example, admits only 20 per cent of its applicants a year, and shares a gender admission policy with an early noughties Yorkie bar. It apparently offers the best standard of education there is, which is obvious from the successes of their famous alumni, like Prince Harry, who was able to retire at just 36.

Despite appearances, I did not go to a private school. Lots of people assume, due to my correct pronunciation of words, choirboy appearance and generally haunted vibe, that I followed a typical Eton-to-Cambridge-to-Comedy pipeline. It is incredibly frustrating to be tarred with the same brush as all the genuine private school dweebs with none of the benefits. They got a top-tier education, a goldmine of connections and the sweet blessing of nepotism, and in exchange, everyone gets to call them pompous twats. That's the trade-off. I didn't get any of that and I'm still labelled a posh wanker. Where's the justice in that?

I am, in actual fact, from the streets. The streets of Harpenden, Hertfordshire, where the schools are all comprehensives, open to everyone. Provided your parents can afford one of the extortionate homes in the catchment area.

So not private, per se, but not as 'state' as it claimed to be. It wasn't like I was being taken out of one of those violent state-school jungles you see on soaps but never quite believe, where students openly sell drugs in the classroom but have to read books behind the bike sheds, for fear someone will catch them. Schools that get a rating of 'good' from an Ofsted inspector who's simply trying not to get stabbed.

My school was somewhere in the middle. We had the occasional teen pregnancy or black eye, sure. But the main thing you had to worry about was returning from the toilet to find your backpack turned inside out and your stuff all over the floor. There was a group from a neighbouring village known as the 'Markyate Boys', who spent their evenings at 'the rec', a field behind a former youth club, in which they would smoke rollies and have sexual experiences much earlier than the rest of us. So snobby were us Harpenden natives that we judged our Markyate friends as being more 'dangerous' based almost entirely on the fact they travelled by bus. Their village was more run-down, underfunded and overdue a revamp, and like most hard-done-by places, the kids there had to grow up much faster. It's a strange curio of Britain that the more stuck in the past an area, the further in their own future the kids live. And we'd gather round them at lunchtime, like members of a remote tribe being shown an iPhone for the first time, to hear their incredible tales of inhaling cannabis, and fingering Gemma.

My kidney holiday happened during primary school, however. A very different prospect to big school. Everyone's a lot more similar in primary school and coming-of-age experiences range from jumping off the top of the climbing frame to licking the metal railing to see what it tastes like. There are a few boys with red rings round their gobs from sucking their own bottom lips too hard, or wearing jumpers that are slightly the wrong shade of grey, but largely, kids in primary school are all the same. The main drama came from fears someone may or may not have cracked their head open, a phenomenon that seemed almost ritualistically frequent in my childhood, but you never hear of today. Were grown-ups letting you get on with it back then? Were floors harder? Or more slippery? Or have children evolved thicker skulls to combat hospital waiting times? Either way – school itself was fine. I didn't hate it at all. But it's still, ultimately, school. Offer me two weeks off from it and I'll give you my left kidney.

After months of tests, a date was finally set for the big op. All week, teachers did their best to explain to my classmates why I would be taking a leave of absence, and on my final day of school for a fortnight, the class presented me with a glittery A3 Good Luck card they had all written thoughtful messages in, such as, 'Good luck,' and, 'Good luck, Rhys.' I said goodbye that afternoon with a feeling of excitement so palpable you'd have thought I was going to space.

Fortuitously enough, Dan was coming round for dinner that day. I had been at his house when I writhed around with the first signs of my internal failure. Everything was falling into place. But when I got home my mum told me the awful news that the operation had been delayed. By three whole months. It might as well have been an entire lifetime. I left Dan to play Crash Team Racing solo while I responded to the bad news by pacing around the house slamming every door over and over again.

Obviously that's a very dramatic response to a can being kicked down the road. You'd think I'd be high on the relief of another cancelled plan, popping Babycham like I'd had a gig cancelled in Montreal. But this wasn't cancelled, it was only delayed. And I'm not so anxious I'd ever hope a hospital sets on fire. When you've spent so long building yourself up to tackle something daunting, expending all that mental energy for nothing, knowing you'll have to do the same thing again in a few months' time, you slam a few doors in frustration, it turns out. Not to mention the humiliation of having to turn up at school on Monday to a group of kids who had spent their entire Friday wishing me well. It was barely long enough to wash off the good luck glitter.

As I eventually sat up in the hospital the night before the operation, I'd have given anything for it to be delayed another three months. And then another. And to keep delaying it three months until I died of old age with 1.1 kidneys inside me. Instead, I had a nosebleed on my dad's shoulder and ruined a new polo shirt he'd claimed was the greatest T-shirt he'd ever bought. So much of my childhood was spent tilting my head back in bathrooms with tissues up my nose as some-one's mum rushed in with some random spurious miracle solution they'd heard about, like placing a wet flannel on your neck or an ice cube in your pocket. Some kids are pre-disposed to nosebleeds, usually at inopportune moments, while finally standing up to a bully or when greeting a bride. Nosebleeds continued long into my teens, culminating in a major one thirty seconds into my final graded A-level theatre performance, as the cast and I desperately scrambled for ways to write the nosebleed into the script. 'Yes, Anne Frank,' I whispered, 'between those Nazis and this nosebleed, it's been a tough couple of weeks.' The examiner told me afterwards we could've stopped and waited to resume the play when I was ready. That doesn't sound very 'yes, and?' to me.

I woke up after my operation on a ward with two boys suf-fering from kidney stones. I found it laughable that they were just trying to get rid of some tiny pebbles, while I had to have my whole kidney removed, the part-timers. That was until I heard exactly how you get rid of kidney stones. We all lay there on drips, unable to move much. For a brief moment, nurses worried my reluctance to eat anything was down to a lack of appetite, but it was actually because I considered the hospital food too exotic, especially as it was all touching on the plate. The NHS didn't have the resources to deal with whatever the hell that issue was, so I ate a lot of toast.

Like a widow, my kidney was still getting used to being alone, and so it wouldn't always remind me to urinate until the very last moment. It was rarely catastrophic, as I was still going in bedpans, usually with the help of my mum, who would look away like a waiter as a customer enters their PIN in the card machine. One evening, when my mum was asleep elsewhere, I turned to a nurse to help me. True to form, the nurse on shift was the one I fancied, and I had been passing the time mentally composing poetry for her. Too embarrassed to let her watch, I informed her I'd been doing this myself this entire time, and all I needed was for her to pass me the receptacle. She drew the curtain and I got to work on a piss that took so long I began to wonder if there was a mix-up and they accidentally put more kidneys in. Mildly embarrassed, I attempted to speed things up, but pretty soon the bedpan became so full I could no longer hold its weight, dropping it all over myself and soaking the bed. If you've ever tried to woo a lady, particularly an older one, you'll know that covering yourself in your own urine has a success rate of 0 per cent. Unless she's much, much older, in which case it's a great way to make her feel less self-conscious about her own shortcomings.

Throughout this whole process, grown-ups obsessively called me brave, but I didn't feel brave at all. I'd been passive in the whole experience. Had I any other option and chosen surgery, maybe there'd be a smidge of courage to acknowledge, but in this instance, some grown-ups told me what had to be done, and I went along with it. It was no different to any other day in my life. When a child is sick, it's the parents who have to be brave. What could be more terrifying than something happening to your own child, and yet *you* are the one who has to put on a brave face so *they* aren't scared. I wasn't brave. Bravery is about choices. Doing something scary that I had to do anyway is just normal life. Far easier to have major surgery than go to a dinner party. At least I get to be unconscious for the first one.

That's the unfortunate thing about my childhood trauma. It's not enough, is it, having a kidney removed? I can't exactly use it for anything. There's no Netflix drama about the dark-souled survivor who lost a kidney when he was nine. I didn't get a dying wish, or a bedside visit from Spider-Man. Just once I'd like to hear, 'Can you believe it, he did all that with one kidney!' But given how little impact it has on anything, that sentence could only be used to describe a particularly translucent piss. I mean, it's not even as useful comedically as Type 1 diabetes. It's nothing. I might as well have had my tonsils out, or currently have piles. No one cares, it's just a mildly interesting thing I can say when playing two truths and a lie. It wasn't even in good enough nick to sell on the black market. What a waste.

Pretty soon I was back at school, refreshed from my break and anticipating at least a bit of attention from my class-mates. Little had changed, of course, except for the fact the boys wanted to see the scar and say the word 'cool'. The main headline was I was now allowed a bottle of water on my desk and could go to the toilet whenever I liked. At the time, these felt like enormous treats, like a VIP table in a club that only I had access to. In hindsight, these are both basic human rights, which I'd paid for with one of my organs. Clean drinking water? Permission to urinate? I understand that giving either of these to all the children would mean constant water fights and endless bunking off in cubicles, but it's a sad indictment of Britain that we have to ration children's pisses. Of course we *want* you to drink water, kids, but only in our dedicated water-drinking hour. And you'd better hope you need the toilet immediately!

While the water bottle on my desk was a treat, it also acted as a big flashing sign that said, 'Different!' Suddenly I was lumped into a category with the boy who had to permanently wear a protective scrum cap after a nasty collision with a lamp post, who I was also forced to play football with for six weeks of break times in an exclusive game, us two fragile dweebs and a single dinner lady. I thought back to all those doctors telling me how normal it was to have one kidney, and how unusual it felt right now. 'But plenty of these kids won't even know they've only got one functioning kidney!' I'd say, in protest. 'They should be playing with us. Or I should be with them.' But nothing. I was stuck watching a fifty-year-old named Sue take penalties against a child in Petr Čech cosplay.

Sports began to fall by the wayside. Football may have just been six weeks on the sidelines, something my Chelsea name-sake would go on to perfect as well. But elsewhere, my mum had been told in no uncertain terms that I was not to partici-pate in karate 'ever again'. A sentence in which 'again' has no real place. Still, you should've seen the tears. Not from me, but from various sensei in the Home Counties. What a loss to the world of martial arts. I never wore a white dressing gown again, out of sheer respect. And fear I might nosebleed all over it.

My dreams of being fly-half for England also lay in a crumpled heap on the floor, as I'm sure I would have too, if I ever actually played rugby. In Year 7, they only allowed 'touch' rugby, where tackles were replaced with pats and the whole game was essentially tag. But by Year 9, schools began to encourage full clatterings during PE, to tire out the pupils so they weren't lucid enough to correct their Business Studies teachers. Praise be, I thought, to have the permanent sick note I had always coveted. No rugby allowed. Doctor's orders. They'll send me to the computer lab to do my homework, I assumed. I won't do it, of course, I'll browse one of the eighteen forums I'm attempting to become custodian of, or learn how to write HTML, or play Jumpers for Goalposts 3. Whatever. I won't be out in the cold getting run into by farmers.

This was a pipe dream. Instead, the PE department decided it was vital for me to get some exercise, and if they had to watch a bunch of teenagers play an abysmal interpretation of rugby, then so did I. At first, I was made to run laps around the pitch like a well-trained dog, or a substitute who never gets called upon. But the coach didn't know what he was dealing with. I have feigned injuries to get out of dancing at social events – do you really think I'm incapable of rolling an ankle for the greater good of avoiding cardio? By week four, I was standing next to the teacher and shouting instructions to my classmates like an assistant coach of a Premier League manager who doesn't speak English, absolutely mad on power. Until a few months later when it got cold, and they let me go to the computer lab.

None of my friends were particularly interested in my rugby absence. They had questions about how my mono-kidney would affect my life, but none of them were to do with contact sports, for which they rightly assumed it changed nothing. Their main query, aged fourteen, was, 'Does it mean you can't drink?' There's something about the final few years before you're legally allowed to drink alcohol that makes you utterly obsessed with drinking as much of it as possible, no more exciting sound than the clinking of bottles in a backpack on the way to a 'revision meet-up' at a friend's house. But having one kidney didn't mean I couldn't drink. It meant I couldn't down dirty pints my mates had dipped their balls in, but that was still just the rugby embargo. Drinking was fine; I abstained out of choice. Not to protect my health, that would be far too logical. Instead, it was to mimic my friend Tom, a footballing prospect, with a neat left foot and a semi-professional contract at a lower-league football team, who had decided to abstain from the sauce to protect his future. Naturally, I used my kidney as an excuse to do the same. Anything you can't do, I can also not do better.

This charade lasted about six months, before Tom stopped showing up at things altogether to focus on football and I realised alcohol offered a handy solution to much of my initial social apprehension, a fact I feel lucky not to have escalated into what's known as 'a problem'. Years later, Tom ironically now works as a nightclub barman, though the thrill of getting one of his special novelty-sized Grey Geese will never match the exclusivity of my sports bottle in Year 5.

So having my kidney out changed almost nothing. Barring annual check-ups at Great Ormond Street until I was fifteen – really an excuse for a day off in London with my mum, in which the check-up would last all of twenty minutes and we'd spend the rest of the day pottering about doing our favourite activity: buying me trainers. I never really saw a doctor about it again. Frankly, I wouldn't mind if those check-ups had continued. I looked forward to those days so much, and not because of the day off school, but the adventure, the sense that we were off to do our special pilgrimage, all because, like most pilgrimages, we went through something ages ago that no longer matters at all. And barely even mattered at the time. It didn't stop me drinking, it didn't stop me getting nosebleeds, and I found out in my twenties, it hadn't even stopped me playing rugby. My mum had made that up to protect me.

My kidney may have failed. I may have failure in my DNA. But could I have done anything differently to stop it happening? According to the doctors, no. Most people use failure as a learning experience, to not repeat the same mistakes again. What am I supposed to do with this lesson? Not be born? Sometimes it's nice to experience a failure that's completely out of your control, not something you're responsible for. To realise that no matter how much you try to plan life, something completely random can happen at any moment to scupper it. That might seem terrifying, but it's something that warms me. Not as much as tipping a bedpan full of piss over myself. But it warms me all the same. We are forever at the mercy of random, unannounced failure. We deal with it when it comes, and that's life. How sweet it is.

Based on a True Story

It's Christmas Eve. A businessman in a pinstripe suit puts down the phone in his office and straightens out some papers on his desk. Outside the door, his secretary types in an unbroken focus. 'Hey, don't work too hard,' comes his voice from above her, snapping her out of it. 'I got you this, to say thank you for another great year.' The boss places a gift-wrapped box down on her desk and takes out his gloves, ready to head off. She looks at the box and smiles. 'Merry Christmas, Caroline,' he says. 'Are you spending it with family?' 'Oh, if I get the time. I have a few things to . . .' she offers, drifting back to her work. 'Well,' smiles the business-man, 'give them my best.'

We cut to Caroline racing through the high street, deter-mined. The cold air smarts as she adjusts her scarf and wraps her coat tighter under her folded arms. Eventually, she reaches a toy shop and heads inside, pulling out a scrap of paper with a long list of unchecked items. She searches desperately, before finally finding the toy she's looking for and racing to the checkout. The queue is enormous, but she joins it, shuf-fling impatiently, checking her watch, eventually reaching the front and grasping for her purse. The clerk informs her, 'This doesn't come with batteries.' 'Oh,' she says, 'I'll take a pack of double A batteries too then, please.' 'We don't sell batter-ies,' he monotones back, chewing his gum obnoxiously loud.

'Right,' she says, taking out her scrap of paper and adding 'batteries' to the list. She pays and runs out of the store in a panic.

She spots a cheap jewellery store, but as she approaches, the manager is locking up. 'Sorry, ma'am, we're closed . . . for Christmas.' She pleads, but it's no use. She heads towards a CD shop as they turn the sign from 'open' to 'closed', and as she arrives at Wacky Mike's Pic N Mix Emporium, he pulls down the shutters. She takes out her list, and for the first time we see all the items on it: candy, CDs, DVDs, bracelet, batteries, light bulbs, yarn, a mop. 'Argh,' she cries, staring up at the sky. 'My family are going to have to go without again this year. Why can't all these items be available under one convenient roof!'

We pan to a man, leaning against a wall, watching Caroline's anguish. He flicks his cigarette and nods, a look of destiny in his eyes. It's clear he has had an idea for a business. And it might just work.

The screen goes black, and on it appears white text that reads: *'Is That Everything?' The Woolworths Story.*
Directed by: Christopher Columbus.

This is the future we're staring down the barrel of: a film depicting the origin story of every business there is or ever has been.

It will come as no surprise, given how many of my references in this book are to vague film clichés, that I am obsessed with movies. Cinema is a go-to hobby for many introverts. It may take place in public, but it can easily be a private and personal experience. Plus, it's one of the few places you're literally not allowed to talk to me. The set-up, with the enormous screen, high volume and low lights, almost necessitates concentration, and is a rare example of somewhere someone other than myself will get angry at me for looking at my phone. It's how they should do school.

Naturally, this experience is almost always ruined by other people. On numerous occasions, I've silently seethed behind Neanderthals disrespecting the etiquette, whether to wikipedia 'Robert Oppenheimer' two hours into the film, or to stretch an arm fully above their tilted-back head to drop popcorn into their open gob from a great height, as Christian Bale does his best to portray Dick Cheney in the background.

I could never go to the cinema to watch a comic-book movie, for example, even if I wanted to, for the fact I'd have to do it surrounded by other people's reactions. A whoop or cheer at the fist of an assumed-dead Avenger bursting through the rubble, or gasps at the actor who used to play this superhero turning up for a lucrative cameo comeback, are enough to ruin the whole thing for me. I am trying to escape the world at the cinema, not gather all its residents around me to make their own *Gogglebox*.

But it's not just the general public that ruin cinema for me. Most recently, I have become exhausted by the modern trend of the 'corporate origin movie' parodied in the opening of this chapter, as cinema continues its desperate pursuit of brand recognition, churning them out faster than hamburgers in *The Founder*. If we've already seen movies telling us how Beanie Babies and Tetris came to be, maybe Woolworths was too realistic an example to highlight how ridiculous this craze is? Perhaps I should've imagined a $100-million-budget K-Y Jelly epic, or Christopher Nolan's *Crocodile Dentist*? Who's to say we won't one day see Austin Butler playing a failed quarterback-cum-entrepreneur who exorcises the demons of his past failures by making sure every man and his dog knows the name Nerf? Frankly, we can't be far away from a movie about the origin of the business origin movie boom.

It started so strong. *The Social Network* came out in 2010, and while it wasn't the first to tell of a mega-corporation's humble beginnings, it was the most impactful in recent memory. Some spoilers ahead for those who haven't yet heard of and formed an opinion about Mark Zuckerberg, but the film tells the story of one plucky Harvard student who beat the odds to become successful, by creating social media platform Facebook. Only, there were two other Harvard students, a pair of hench twins both played by now disgraced Armie Hammer, who thought Facebook was their idea. Plus a third guy who looks like Spider-Man who thinks he owns it too, and Justin Timberlake as the founder of Napster, who can expect a spin-off business origin movie of his own any day now. It's brilliant and compelling and barely scratches the surface of a genuine business behemoth. *The Social Network* went on to win three Oscars and four Golden Globes. Facebook went on to expose the media illiteracy of seventy-year-olds and become a cutting edge platform for memes from nine years ago.

Next came *Jobs*, a 2013 film about Steve Jobs founding Apple, in which the costume department must've worked a cumulative total of four minutes. Told through flashbacks at one of his iconic keynote addresses, it paints a picture of a man hell-bent on turning his business selling niche, colourful monitors for quirky graphic designers into creating the thing most people in the Western world will stare at most frequently throughout their lives, the iPhone.

Similarly, with 2016's *The Founder* we're told the story of how a small, family-run village burger chain went on to become McDonald's when a local businessman redesigned it

as a real-estate business that simply 'housed' fast-food res-
taurants, once again allowing us the privilege of seeing two
brothers get absolutely fucked over by someone even more
sociopathic than they are, as in *The Social Network*. I await
the Tate brothers biopic with bated breath, or perhaps *Valen-
cia: A Tale of Two Nevilles*.

My opinion on these films is irrelevant. The point is not
whether business origin films are good, it's whether they are
necessary. For each of the above examples, the answer is yes.
As much as any art can be deemed 'necessary'.

Facebook, Apple and McDonald's are culture-defining,
everyday-life-altering, consequential businesses that don't
just have a place in our society, but have moulded it into a
new shape entirely. How we communicate and consume
media has been changed for ever by Facebook and Apple.
The erosion of our own attention spans, willpower, ability to
resist temptation could be put down to a combination of all
three. Even more simple things, like the disappearance of
buttons from our screens, is down to Apple, and from our
trousers, McDonald's. They aren't simply iconic logos, but
socially embedded platforms on which we live our daily lives.
And they're still growing, continuing to dominate, evolve
and alter us in the process. Films about their *origins* don't go
nearly far enough.

Beanie Babies were a brief trend in the nineties. Tetris is a
2D computer game no one plays any more.

How did we get *WeCrashed*, a TV show about the office-
space rental business WeWork, before we got *The Social
Network 2*? *The Social Network 1* ends with Mark Zuckerberg refreshing a Facebook homepage layout that now looks
like a newspaper from the 1950s. The film is centred around
what is now probably Facebook's fifth most significant court

case. They should be turning *The Social Network* into the new *Fast and Furious* and making ten of them. My only advice would be to drop the 'The'. Just *Social Network*. It's cleaner.

Obviously, a story can still be relevant and enthralling without having to have transformed the way we all live. That's basically what all films are. But when it comes to the origin story of a business, there's a lot of heavy lifting to do to make us root for a millionaire who had a great idea of how to become a billionaire. In most cases, we're asked to punch our fists in the air in that Hollywood 'we did it!' style because a few men have come to a lucrative contractual agreement. It's the modern 'will-they-won't-they?', but instead of 'will they kiss and live happily ever after?' it's 'will they sign on the dotted line and make $800 million?'. It's only a matter of time before they go full romcom and release *(500) Days of Solvency* and *Bridget Jones's Diary of a CEO*.

Supposedly this is because they're relatively cheap to make, mostly consisting of conversations in boardrooms, have a built-in marketing shortcut of a recognisable name, and, some claim, already have intrinsic stakes. But what stakes are there in a story we already know the ending of? It's difficult to feel the vice-grip tension of a thriller while watching *Air*, the film about whether Michael Jordan will choose Nike to produce his line of sneakers, while sitting in the cinema wearing Nike Air Jordans. And this is how far through the Yellow Pages we've got already. *Air* isn't even the origin story of a business, it's the story of that business's sub-business. We're months away from seeing *George: An Asda Epic*.

Once, we had thrilling, heartfelt biopics of individuals, from odds-defying athletes to genius artists battling their own circumstances; now, we turn to biopics of corporations themselves, or the various men who stole the ideas for them. Now, we're asking Eva Longoria to direct a film about the origin of the Flamin' Hot Cheeto. That isn't a joke, it's called *Flamin' Hot* and has a Rotten Tomatoes score of 67 per cent. So that's where we are. Desperate Housewives are making crisps movies. What's worse, an *LA Times* investigation concluded that the supposedly inspiring story of the man who created the spicy crisp flavour isn't even true. I haven't seen it. I've tried the crisps. Sure, they're delicious, but I've never bitten into any snack and immediately thought: 'I'd like a hundred-and-ten-minute rundown of how these came to be.' I'm not Jerry Seinfeld.

I'm not a critic, nor do I believe in them. And in some cases I've loved the films I'm referring to. But it feels quite a dystopian trend to get our heartfelt, against-the-odds stories through the successes of corporations, rather than individuals. Have we lost our appetite for human endeavour entirely? Where's the invention and the creativity in making a movie from the Wikipedia page of a corporation? If anything, Eva Longoria should be applauded for not reading beyond the page title.

Sometimes I wish my life could be run like a company. Life as an individual is tough. We all face big decisions, but in the end, it's the most emotionally invested – and often irrational – person who has to make them: us. If and when we get them wrong, there's no one else to blame but ourselves. I, for one, think it would be nice to relinquish autonomy completely for a while and let a board of emotionally unattached experts vote on my movements. Surely they know better than I do? After all, I am a business, in a sense. I am a product. People spend their money and they get me. Am I so different from a packet of spicy Wotsits?

That's why I've decided to write my life as a movie. To detach myself completely, and see it objectively from the outside. Sure, it's unlikely to be a box office hit, even if I were to cast myself as a CGI monkey. And sure, I've taken a leaf out of Eva Longoria's book, stretching the truth and imagining a fictional future. But as long as it says 'based on a true story' at the start, I think it holds up legally. And who cares if it doesn't? I'm not going to file a lawsuit against myself. Roll opening credits.

FUNNYBALL

ACT ONE

A small boy who hasn't yet grown into his face sits alone in the school cafeteria, sketching. He's in the zone, oblivious to the noise around him, when his only friend, Jonah Hill, sits down opposite, talking about how a girl he likes has noticed him for the first time. The boy doesn't hear him. Jonah Hill snatches the paper off the boy and asks what he's drawing, instantly noticing how 'sick' and 'dope' it is, asking why the boy never shows anyone. 'They're just for me,' the boy says, 'I don't care what anyone thinks of them.'

Jonah Hill scoffs. 'That's what people say when they suck at stuff. Girls will love this shit!'

But the boy doesn't care. He takes the drawing back and slides it into his folder, when suddenly the school's henchest jock walks past, pushing the folder onto the floor, spilling the papers everywhere. It's not just drawings, but poems, stories, lyrics, everything. 'What are you working on, bitch,' says the bully, 'your lame little Head Boy speech?' The boy scrambles to pick up the papers but the bully gets to one first. It's a perfect sketch of their classmate, Wendy. 'Oh shit,' says the bully, but before he can tell anyone, Jonah Hill snatches it back and sends him on his way. The bully departs, laughing.

'I can't believe you're running for Head Boy,' says Jonah Hill. The boy explains that it's good for his CV and university applications. 'Sure,' replies Jonah, 'but did you know you had to do a speech when you signed up?'

The entire year group gather in the school hall, ready for student hustings. The Head Boy candidates sit on the stage, awaiting their turn to speak at the lectern. The boy is set to go last. Everyone who steps up is met with rapturous applause, trading on their pre-existing popularity and all parrotting the same identical crowd-pleasing promises of extra days off and more relaxed uniform rules. Finally, it's the turn of the boy. 'Last but not least,' introduces the head teacher, to snickers, as the audience nudge each other in anticipation. As the boy steps up, the shrill ringing of microphone feedback reverberates around the room, despite the fact it's the exact same microphone all the other kids used, and this didn't happen for any of them.

'In the beginning,' he says, to bemused faces, 'God created the heavens and the Earth. In the meantime, Millford Park School created the common room and the kitchenette.' A few members of the crowd let out genuine chuckles, as jocks nudge them to shut up. 'God soon went on to create dry land, waters, plants, animals, Mr Clifford, infernos, everything,' continues the boy, to increasing laughter. 'Millford, however, came to a stand-still.' The audience shuffle forward in their seats. This isn't like the other speeches. 'For years, students have settled for a plain common room, a shoddy kitchenette, comfy chairs which were torn apart and then removed and then given back and then removed again. A sense of lull fell over the school, a sense of boredom which no Head Boy could fix.

'This was all until God sent down himself in human form. A saviour was born, the Messiah had arrived, and with a controversial speech, a blue tie and a very slim chance, he introduced himself . . . "Hello, I'm Rhys," he said.'

The crowd erupt, laughing and applauding at the entirely original and ingenious idea to parody a Bible chapter. No one has ever done anything like this before, and as the speech continues, plagiarising lines from *The Mighty Boosh* and using the phrase 'Rhysus Christ' seven times, they're fully won round. Rhys catches eyes with Jonah, leaning in the doorway at the back of the hall. He nods back proudly.

After the speeches, everyone wants a piece of Rhys, coming over to congratulate him and tell him he should be a stand-up comedian. 'Oh no, comedians are all old fogeys in their thirties and forties,' he says back, but they keep insisting he is more than funny enough, and would be the breath of fresh air the entire scene is crying out for. As the crowd parts conveniently, an attractive (to Rhys, who is also her age) girl approaches. She looks familiar. Like a drawing.

'Well done, Rhys, that was sensational, and really fit.'

Rhys's heart races. 'You . . . you know my name?' he stutters.

'Of course. It's Rhysus Christ, right?'

Later that evening, Rhys and Jonah Hill are watching TV. 'I told you people would like you if you let them see how talented you are,' says Jonah Hill. 'Imagine how many friends and girlfriends you could have if you were an actual stand-up comedian.' Rhys bats this away, repeating his line about how all comedians are old. 'That's it!' says Jonah. 'That's your business model. What if there was a comedian, but *young*.'

Rhys stares at the TV. A middle-aged man in a suit performs stand-up comedy before introducing another middle-aged man in a suit to do the same.

Once Jonah Hill has gone home, Rhys googles his favourite comedian and sees that he got discovered in open mic contests, which landed him a top agent. Intrigued, he fills out a competition entry form before slamming the laptop shut as though he's scared of it.

ACT TWO

Part One

'Wow, was that your first gig?' comes the voice of the MC, as he packs down the mic stand.

'Third, actually,' corrects Rhys, proudly.

'Same difference. You're incredible, and the breath of fresh air the entire scene has been crying out for.'

Rhys has taken the plunge and begun performing stand-up comedy, mostly in venues he has to show a fake ID to even enter, accompanied by Jonah Hill, who he runs all his joke ideas by. We see in montage a variety of gigs to a variety of audiences, from two people to twelve people, from the upstairs of pubs to the downstairs of pubs. They high-five as Rhys comes off-stage over and over again, only occasionally swapping celebration for consolation when Jonah Hill has to put an arm around Rhys's shoulder. They laugh on trains while writing in notepads, negotiate with bouncers and collect tens of open mic comics' business cards. 'You Make My Dreams' by Hall & Oates plays.

Back at school, they check the results of the student elections on the noticeboard. Rhys has not won Head Boy, but they both shrug. Who cares about that, when they're already on to bigger things? They head off to the computer lab to browse the website of their upcoming summer excursion to Tanzania. Jonah Hill waxes lyrical about how he can't wait to experience the culture and wildlife, and welcomes the physical and mental challenge of doing something so brand new, life-enriching and horizon-broadening. It's truly going to be the trip of a lifetime, and he gets to do it with his best friend in the whole world. It couldn't be more perfect. Rhys is excited too. Partly because it's great for the CV and universities love that sort of stuff. But also because there'll be such exciting things to sketch and write about there.

But what's this? Rhys has a new email. It's the open mic competition he entered after googling his favourite comedian. He's been competing in the heats already. Oh my God! Rhys has been accepted into the semi-final! This is huge. He hugs Jonah Hill as they jump around with pure glee, until Jonah Hill notices the date of the contest. 'July 15th? But that's when we go to Africa.' They both come crashing down to Earth. Why can't anything ever be convenient? 'I guess you can enter again next year,' says Jonah Hill, adamant that Rhys wouldn't throw away the trip of a lifetime for the sake of an open mic competition. But Rhys has had a taste of it now, and he wants everything right away. Plus, will he even still be the *young* comedian next year? This was Jonah Hill's business idea to begin with.

Over the next few months, the pair drift. Rhys is going to gigs alone, and Jonah Hill is getting on with his own stuff, shopping for hiking gear, trying to impress groups of girls. They're still friends, but it's not quite the same. There's tension between them.

Rhys experiences his first lows. Gigs go badly, jokes stop

working, bouncers stop asking for ID. When doing a corporate gig for a pension company, he is forced to share a tiny, windowless dressing room with two acrobatic dancers, who swing in metal rings above the audience during dinner, wearing nothing but underwear and feather boas. When they return to the dressing room, they loudly discuss how they both currently have the viral infection mumps. Rhys frantically googles whether the mumps vaccine is given out at school, and even types out a message to Jonah Hill to ask, but deletes it.

Days later he has an exciting meeting with a TV producer, but is disheartened to hear the producer is sceptical. 'A comedian . . . but *young*? It won't work. You'll never be successful, buddy.'

Rhys is taken aback. 'Never? If the issue is just that I'm young, surely I could be successful in the future?' he replies.

'You young people with your slang. I'll never understand it. Never!'

Eventually the day comes. Jonah Hill stands at airport departures, looking at a boarding screen that says 'Tanzania'. He checks his phone for a message from Rhys. Nothing. Rhys stands backstage at a comedy club, checking his phone for a good luck text from Jonah Hill. Nada.

After a deep breath, Rhys walks on-stage, and before we know it, he's in a swanky agency office being chatted up by a room full of 55-year-olds wearing Yeezys. 'I've never seen anything like it. A comedian . . . but *young*. It's a genius business idea. How did you come up with it?' The entire office nod and hum in agreement. 'We want to sign you, but we've got to do something about that name.' Rhys seems confused. 'We like Rhys. But drop the Jones. Rhys *James*. It's cleaner.'

With his new backers, Rhys hits the mainstream. 'Rhys

James' posters line the streets of the Edinburgh Fringe Festival. Fans queue for selfies, newspapers spin into frame with five-star reviews, calling Rhys 'the breath of fresh air the entire scene was crying out for'. He climbs the ladder, landing TV gigs, talk show appearances and important podcasts (sparkling, poppadoms, Angel Delight). He even locks eyes with a girl, who we see subtly go from sitting in the crowd to standing in the wings.

But something is due to go wrong, and pretty soon, more newspapers spin into frame, with headlines that read: 'James the Thief', 'Not in My James' and, so the audience are certain, 'Rhys James Sued Over Business Origin by Former Friend'. Someone called Jonah Hill is claiming to have invented Rhys James several years ago, when he first suggested the idea of a comedian, but young.

Things seem sad for a moment, until Rhys shows his ruthless streak by hiring the most vicious lawyers in the business. He enters courtrooms wearing sunglasses and things go so well he leaves the courtroom wearing even bigger sunglasses. His lawyers high-five in fits of laughter, as the bus Jonah Hill waits for drives through a puddle and splashes him.

In montage, Rhys stands on-stage as the camera spins around him in a perfect circle. Every time it goes behind him, we see the venues get larger and larger, and every time it goes in front, his face is older and older. As time goes on, Rhys releases a smash hit book, directs smash hit but still artistically lauded films, and hosts the world's most successful virtual reality podcast, in which *you* are the guest. Between commitments, he takes his phone out to reject social invitations. His smile even begins to fade as he becomes jaded with age. Almost against his will, he has become an absolute star, far eclipsing anything anyone could ever have predicted.

People worship the ground he walks on. He's finally Rhysus Christ.

Part Two

Rhys, now forty-seven, enters his mansion through the main lobby of the East Wing, and heads into the drawing room. Awards line the walls. A cat slaloms between Rhys's legs. The whole place has the distinct feel of no children living in it. He has everything he ever wanted, and nothing he didn't ever want. Yet, on a rare night off, he can't quite figure out what to do with himself. His phone no longer buzzes with invitations, and he feels a sharp pang of loneliness. He wants to be wanted, he just doesn't want anyone to expect anything of him. 'I suppose that isn't a unique position,' he thinks to himself.

'Why don't you take up a hobby like me?' says Rhys's stunning life-partner, gesturing to her easel and paintbrush. 'It's a great way to unwind.' Rhys dismisses this idea. When your job is creative, creative hobbies don't so much unwind you as stress you out further. They say find a job you love and you'll never work a day in your life. The reality is, doing something you love, you'll never get a day off. It's not such a great way to unwind when your own thoughts have become work.

Rhys looks through his phone contacts for a friend to hang out with, but they're all colleagues, people who work for him, or people he works for. Scorsese? No. Gerwig? No. Gamble? Definitely not. It dawns on him that he doesn't have any actual friends. In fact, he explains, 'The last real friend I had tried to sue me for stealing his business idea.'

'What was the business idea?' asks his gorgeous and intellectually buxom partner.

'I was,' he deadpans.

As she heads out for the evening, Rhys looks up Jonah Hill on social media. It seems he is now a teacher-scientist-nurse-fireman, who is the most fulfilled person in the world, not given to materialism, doing things he finds noble because he enjoys helping others. Growing jealous, and in a moment of weakness, Rhys opens up a new tab to google himself. The praise he finds upon doing so bounces off him entirely, and he digs deeper, searching for pain. He types in his old name, before he was told to change it, and discovers one disgruntled commenter, claiming they went to school with Rhys, and he was an absolute bastard. In fact, they point specifically to a speech he made when running for Head Boy, in which he said the now completely unacceptable slur: 'Vegans are pussies.' It sparks a vague memory in his head, and a mild panic in his chest. He clicks on their profile to see the entire account is dedicated to spreading this story, and it's getting traction as people ask for more information. He slams the laptop shut as though he's scared of it, and tries to go to sleep.

The next morning, Rhys receives a call from his manager, asking if he knows anything about the 'vegan pussies' accusations. Several of his upcoming TV appearances have been contacted about it, and while they're unproven claims, unlikely to be true, they don't want to take the risk of bringing any negative press to their fledgling platforms. The pile-on snowballs. The public find Rhys particularly fun to bring down, given his droll, smug stage persona. Before long, Rhys is without work entirely. No one in the industry will touch him, and people online continue to speculate on what else he might've said in that speech. 'Apparently he called recycling "gay".' 'I heard he used to drink milk from a *cow*!' None of it is true, but it doesn't matter.

Rhys spirals into a full, public mental breakdown. He starts therapy, but his therapist records their meetings and publishes them online. He vents on a private blog, but this gets discovered and circulated everywhere. People think these are all PR operations to trick the public into sympathising with the poor millionaire, but it isn't. Rhys's publicist dropped him long ago. His agents, now 75-year-olds wearing Sambas, eventually call him to say it's over. 'When we signed you, we were excited about the prospect of a new business venture. A comedian . . . but young. It was genius. And it made us all a lot of money. But you're not that any more. You're not young, and you're not a comedian. You're a monster. An old monster.'

Rhys hits rock bottom. He walks into a dive bar and orders a strong glass of alcohol. At the next table, two women loudly discuss the Bechdel test.

ACT THREE

Weeks later, Rhys receives an email from a name he half recognises. Wendy Collins. Isn't that the girl from school? 'Thought you might like to see this,' reads the message. Opening the attachment, Rhys sees a video of himself onstage in his school hall. He can't believe how young he looks compared to the others, like when a teenage boy is forced to let his younger brother play football with him and his friends. If only he'd had the wherewithal at the time, he thinks, to reference it in his speech, he might've won. His eyes dampen as he watches the footage, growing emotional as he realises that, in many ways, he's rewatching his very first gig. All of a sudden it gets to the line in question. 'Vegans are pussies!' comes a voice, prompting gasps from the already liberal audience. But it isn't his voice. The camera pans to the back of the room, to reveal Jonah Hill.

That's right! He's the one who shouted it out as a joke, after Rhys had promised dairy alternatives in the canteen. 'I think what Jonah Hill means is that he's never actually seen a . . . vegan,' quips Rhys, quick as a flash, like Jimmy Carr . . . but *young*. The audience laugh, a bit quieter than he remembered, but it relieves the tension nevertheless.

This is it, thinks Rhys. This clears my name! I'm back! He copies the link, ready to post it on social media, but he hesitates for a second. This would bury Jonah Hill. No one's going to hire a teacher, nurse, fireman or scientist who once said V words are P words. He'll be ruined, and he's the most fulfilled man in the world.

SIX MONTHS LATER

Rhys walks through a packed theatre. His cap is low so as not to be spotted by the crowd. He sneaks through the door at the side of the stage and paces up to Dressing Room 1 confidently. Instead of entering, he knocks tentatively before opening the door to reveal a 48-year-old Jonah Hill sitting in front of the mirror. 'Hello, old friend,' he says.

Jonah Hill sighs nervously and straightens out his papers. 'I don't know how you do this performing stuff,' Jonah stutters. 'Mine's just a TED Talk, and I'm still terrified.'

'Oh, you'll be golden,' replies Rhys. 'If in doubt, use my old opening line.'

The lights in the auditorium go down and the audience cheer in anticipation. Rhys leans on the doorway at the back of the room, like Jonah Hill did during the Head Boy speech all those years ago. Music booms and a voice of God announces today's keynote speaker. Jonah Hill walks onstage to rapturous applause, thanks the organisers, and delivers an opening line so devastatingly hilarious, the audience actually turn to each other to shake hands in celebration of their decision to come here today. Rhys pulls his cap lower and walks off into the night. His work here is done.

Back home, Rhys's mansion is now covered in canvases. Paintings of scenery and animals. Sketches of buildings and flowers. Framed poems sit on shelves that once housed awards. He sits at his desk, sketching something new, when his emotionally voluptuous common-law wife enters his office. Instinctively, he hides his drawing with his body, not letting her see it. 'Come on, show me,' she says, and he nervously relents.

It's her. It's perfect. She loves it.

The screen fades to black and the text reads as follows:

Rhys James sold ten million tickets in his very first year performing stand-up. He was the first comedian in history to be young.

He now has his own line of tequila, flavour of crisps and social network.

Directed by Francis Ford Coppola

Starring Daisy Ridley as Rhys James

Dev Patel as Jonah Hill

and

Sydney Sweeney as 'Life Partner'

The End.

To Dare Is to Do

Is there anything more fruitless than trying to rationalise why you like something? As a kid, liking things is seen for what it is, a visceral urge, a sensation. If you ask a child why they like their dog, they'll say because he's brown and friendly and funny. But that's not really *why*, it's just a description of his traits. A bit like as an adult, if you're forced to explain why you love your partner, in a Valentine's card, bespoke vows, deposition or whatever, you reel off a bunch of things that make them a good person, but don't necessarily account for your feelings. 'Oh, she's kind, and we share the same out-look on life.' 'He makes me laugh, and he's got quite the arse.' But these traits aren't unique to your partner, so it can't be as simple as that. If you love someone, you should be completely tongue-tied by that question. Explaining why you *don't* like something is much easier, because you can pinpoint the cause of your rage or disappointment. But to say why I love my girl-friend? Impossible. She's funny, caring, pragmatic, creative and, yes, fit. But those are just adjectives. The reality is, the feeling I get when I'm around her isn't like the feeling I get when I'm around other people. What is that feeling? Fuck off. I don't know, OK. I just love her and there's nothing I can do about it. Christ.

This is what it's like to support a football team. A com-pletely irrational, impossible-to-justify feeling that, in some ways, you wish wasn't there. Often, it's also not even your choice, but a case of geographical coincidence or the decision of one of your elder relatives, passing on their fandom like heart disease. Unlike a dog, or a wife, however, I hate football as much as I love it. The pain it causes me is unsubtle, frequent and expensive. But there's very little I can do about it now. It's there. Part of me. Regardless of how illogical it is, it has been one of the few constants in my life, and one of the key driving forces for me leaving the house.

My family's genetic disease is Tottenham Hotspur. Despite my brother's brief flirtation with Manchester United's golden generation, beguiled by David Beckham's versatile hair and harbouring a secret desire to ever be able to celebrate, us Joneses were all trained to support Spurs from birth. It starts with my gransha (a weird word used in the Welsh valleys for 'grandad') though my dad claims he influenced the whole thing with a contagious childhood enthusiasm for Jimmy Greaves. My gransha has no real links to North London as a Welsh coal miner, though toiling away at the same thing over and over again for little to no reward is the Tottenham way, so maybe it was in his bones?

In the sixties, when my family's collective fandom properly began, Spurs were one of the best teams in the world, winning the domestic double and the European Cup Winners' Cup, and thus marking the worst attempt at 'glory hunting' in history from my elders. Until this year, my thirty-odd years of consciously supporting this team had seen us win exactly one (1) Worthington Cup and one (1) Carling Cup. Those are the same tournament. During a particularly drab and predictable period of Antonio Conte's sulky management in 2022, my brother suggested that by watching Spurs we were effectively spending £100 a week to see a play we hated over and over again, all because my dad liked one of the actors in it over sixty years ago. Then, out of nowhere, one of the new 'cast' scored a last-minute winner to reel us right back into the delusion.

It hooks you in young, football. I have visceral memories of TVs being wheeled into the school hall an hour before lessons to let us watch England in the 2002 World Cup. These days, they recommend you start your day with direct exposure to sunlight and delay caffeine for two hours. Back then, we simply watched Ronaldinho lob David Seaman from a forty-yard free kick that may or may not have been a cross, and immediately got on with eight hours of Year 6.

My life as a football fan began properly on Christmas morning, 2001, when under the tree sat two giant boxes. As we all know, a child's excitement level for a gift is in direct proportion to that gift's size, which is stupid, given the dimensions of a Gameboy, or a cheque. It's so incredibly tantalising to wonder what treasures could possibly fill such an enormous space. A bike? A Wendy house? A novelty-sized cheque? The possibilities are endless!

The tactic of parents here is to keep that box until last, like a festival headliner, but all that serves to do is rush the opening of the other gifts, treating them all as disposable, while the main present looms large. 'Oh sure, this is the exact CD I asked for, and this new T-shirt suits me perfectly. Oh yeah, a satsuma and 50p never go amiss, and I did for some reason really want a toy of a man whose arms you can stretch out really far, but who does literally nothing else, absolutely. But what's in the box? Don't make me put on my best Brad Pitt in *Se7en* voice here, Mum. What's in the *fucking box*?'

And so, after my brother and I raced through the chore of opening several thoughtfully chosen smaller presents curated for our own interests, it was finally time for the big boy. We clawed at our boxes like itchy cricketers, pried open the top and pulled out what awaited us . . . A slightly smaller box. OK. Classic. Lovely gag from Mum and Dad there, though Dad certainly seemed more pleased with himself. Of course, my older brother unwrapped faster than me, so to avoid spoilers was slowed down by my parents as I struggled to keep up, somehow diminishing the magic for everyone. Second box opened, and yep, you guessed it, another marginally smaller box inside. As yet unaware of the concept of Russian dolls, we compared this to 'pass the parcel without the passing', until eventually we got down to one tiny box in the middle. With every smaller box, a new gift had been ruled out. OK, so it's not a bike. Fine. Could be a puppy? Nope. Not a puppy, certainly not with this many impenetrable air-locked layers of cardboard. Could still be a Super Soaker? Negative. Too light. Tamagotchi? Already have one of those, but my parents would've said that before they had me, and look how that turned out. Then, at last, it was the final box. We unwrapped this one slowly out of respect for the presentation and found inside a small leather booklet, about three inches by two. We looked at the booklets, then at each other, and uttered the three words every parent wants to hear about their main extravagance on Christmas morning: 'What is it?'

What it is, is a death sentence. It's a lifetime of self-enforced heartache and universal mockery. Sure, it's also a bonding cheat code and an adrenaline shortcut. But at what cost? In this moment I don't know any of that, all I know is it's a little book of tickets with my name and a cockerel on it. A half-season ticket for Spurs for each of us. Dad and Gransha have them too. Five months later, Tottenham go on to finish the season ninth and we watch from the gods as they lose the league cup final in Cardiff. I'm hooked for life.

My dad is not an angry man. My temper and ability to find the negative in everything, to feel personally wronged and constantly hard done by, are entirely my own. His dad, my gransha, could make a case for possessing the same sort of impotent comical rage I do, once getting sent off for swearing at the referee during a match in which he was the linesman. Maybe it skips a generation, but my dad certainly doesn't have it. During a period of about four years where he became the butt of every single family joke, particularly during meals, he never once snapped, just sighed and attempted to give it back, culminating in him uttering the immortal words, 'Oh, of course, take the piss out of Dad because it's food time,' only to be ribbed even more mercilessly for forgetting the word 'dinner'. So I'm incredibly grateful to 'The Football'™ for allowing me to see the more human side of him, as he seethes at our team's incompetence and rants about inconsequential micro-decisions in the car on the way home.

That's not to say he isn't an optimist. He absolutely is. Perennially convinced he needs to buy the latest kit, because this will be the year it happens, expecting a win from every game regardless of the opponent. When I pessimistically bat these wishes away with cold hard stats and trademark cynicism, he rolls his eyes, pitying my resignation. Conversely, I pity his disappointment at full-time, wondering how he could go in with such high expectations given all the evidence before him.

He once took me to a game early, only explaining when we arrived that for some reason, we had been given the opportunity to walk down to the dugout and meet the manager,

Martin Jol. This is practically unheard of, particularly for a team like Tottenham, for whom managers usually require maximum security to protect them from their own fans' ire. As we walked down the steps towards the big Dutchman, I thought about what I might say to him. About how he'd transformed our style of play into something enjoyable to watch and how much that meant to me as a lifelong Spurs fan. I was fifteen. When we arrived at his feet, my dad launched into a full appraisal: 'Martin, it's great to meet you. I've been a Spurs fan my whole life, and I want to say how impressed I am with the job you're doing. The style of play is the best it's been for years and it's showing in the results. The atmosphere from the fans is incredible, and we're really hopeful this is the year we can do something special.' The colour drained from my face. Leave some meat on the bone, Dad, for crying out loud. There's nothing left! What am I supposed to say? I like your jacket? My dad shook Mr Jol's hand and delivered his final line. 'Thanks for taking the time to speak with us. This is my son, Rhys.' The big Dutch brute turned to look at me, sticking out his giant mitt for me to shake. I had nothing. Everything had been said three seconds ago. I shook Martin's hand, looked in his eyes, and squeaked out one single word . . . 'Brilliant.' Pathetic.

Our season tickets at Tottenham's former stadium White Hart Lane were next to two middle-aged London geezers who'd always arrive after we had, ready to greet us the exact same way. 'Afternoon,' from one of them, 'How are ya?' from the next. Handshake from the first guy, slightly too close shuffle past from the second, holding a blue plastic corner-shop bag he never opened and wearing the same old fleece that smelled not unpleasantly of yoghurt.

There's something quite magical about the football that

means you never technically introduce yourself to anyone. I sat next to these men every other week for the best part of fifteen years, they watched me grow up, and we never once told each other our names. A foreigner trying to learn English would assume they were called 'Afternoon' and 'How are ya?' based on our conversations, and if I hadn't one day overheard 'How are ya?' say the phrase, 'Les, you wanker,' and 'Afternoon' reply, 'Piss off, Nige,' I'd say those were a solid guess.

But somehow, we knew each other. I knew them well enough to know that every time our goalkeeper caught the ball, Les would shout, 'Roll it, roll it, roll it,' while pointing at our right back, only for the goalie to hoof it up the field and Les to say, 'That's the one.' When Stephen Carr returned to Spurs, now a Newcastle player, Les spent the entire game shouting, 'Fred, remember when you used to have pace?' before turning to us for support, mumbling, 'He must hear me, he must be able to, he *must* hear me,' again and again. I also knew that Nige was the wit of the double act, once getting one of the longest terrace laughs I've ever heard for noticing the opposition substitutes warming up in Waitrose-sponsored bibs and coming out with the pithy line: 'Delivering the shopping, boys?' Even at twelve I was aware Waitrose's delivery partner was Ocado, and so the joke didn't hold up. That didn't stop me laughing along with everyone else, of course.

What this means is that they probably knew us too, even if they didn't know our names. They knew we were a family, or you'd have hoped they'd have phoned the police. They knew that I could muster little else than to parrot back their own greetings to them every week. That both my brother and I dropped a few more Ts and Hs while chatting to them. They knew that from the ages of eighteen to twenty-one I believed betting on who would score first was a foolproof get-rich-quick scheme (soon to be replaced by entering the *Dickinson's Real Deal* text-in contest every day for three years). And they also knew that my dad was more of the 'tut-and-shake-your-head' fan, than a flailing-arms obscenity screamer.

That was, until one fateful day, during a match in which the home fans felt particularly aggrieved by the ref. Every little decision was going the other way, from marginal off-sides to fifty-fifty challenges, to stolen half-yards of free kicks being jobs-worthily pulled back, just for our team. While the entire crowd around us were letting their feelings known, Dad stayed firm, folding his arms, rolling his eyes, taking the moral high ground. But every man has his limits. Eventually, a ball went out of play right in front of us, and the ref called it for the other team. Enough was enough. My father stood for the first time all match. I half expected the momentum to lift me up in tandem, in some form of unspoken permission to release my inhibitions like the rest of the crowd. But on this occasion, the rest of the crowd did nothing. Barely even a peep. Maybe the decision was too minor to bother them? Or perhaps the ref had got it right this time? It didn't matter either way. It was too late. Dad was already taken by reckless abandon, up on his feet, pointing an accusatory finger as heads around him turned to look. Words fired out of his mouth like bullets, piercing through the atmosphere. Visceral, furious, spontaneous. 'Ref, you . . . are a cunt!'

Boom. Years' worth of pent-up frustration, released like an overdue radiator bleed. A bus exhaling at its stop. Everyone around us chuckled at this uncharacteristic outburst, particularly given the slight hesitation as he reached for the slam. What it lacked in the touchline wit of a 'Do you want to borrow my glasses, ref?', it more than made up for in shock value. And we didn't have to worry about comic timing – Nige had us covered, following up the outburst with the narratively impenetrable: 'He *must* hear you.'

This is what football can do to a person. It's often claimed that football is used by men as a sort of speed-run for emotions, handily letting out a wide range of them in one neat ninety-minute weekly package, ready to return to their everyday lives as stoic, blank-faced robots until the next match. While this view is archaic, I do think one of the big unspoken appeals of sport is that you not only get to feel a number of extremes, you also know exactly *why* you're feeling them. One of life's biggest frustrations is having a feeling you can't pinpoint to anything specific. We're intrinsically designed to try to find the root cause of every problem, but what if you feel depressed with no valid reason? What if you're just sad, or angry, or scared? Failure to answer that question is what held back mental health discourse for decades, but luckily, through all that, we had football.

Good old football. You feel it all and you know exactly why in each moment. The emotion and the therapy are all rolled into one, and you don't even have to chat to some bell end in a turtleneck. Unless you support Chelsea. Why am I livid? Because the ref's a wanker. Why am I sad? See previous answer. Why am I happy? Because the European teenager I've pinned all my hopes and dreams on has put one past the group of strangers I've decided are my own personal enemies. Simple, conclusive answers.

This is why people really hate VAR. It's not that it's inconsistent or not up to scratch technologically. It's not that it takes too long, slowing down the game. These are false intellectualisations of what's really going on. It's because it nullifies a feeling you felt in the moment and makes you look stupid for feeling it. It's a saving-face nightmare.

Obviously there's a positive flip-side to that, like when a goal your team concedes is overruled. But all that does is lift you from despair, back to default. Far more dramatic is your elation, in all its uncontrollable screams, fist pumps and hugs with your neighbour, being immediately proven to be a mistake. All for nothing. The jumbo screen might as well say: *Checking: Possible Unjustified Joy. Result: Happiness – Overturned.* I genuinely believe no one would have a problem with VAR if they kept it exactly as it is, but rebranded it as: 'And now it's time for . . . the *RANDOMISER!*' VAR already behaves like a wacky game-show feature masquerading as objective truth, so lean into it as nonsense. I, for one, would like to see post-match interviews with players saying things like: 'Yeah, obviously today we've been done by the randomiser, but we go again.' That's football.

VAR isn't the only thing spoiling the emotions. Football fans notoriously rage at the 'part-timers' who join in with the England fervour deep into an international tournament once we've reached the knockout stages and 'Football's Coming Home' is back in the charts. You'd think fanatics of anything would want everyone to appreciate the same thing they do, to see it from their perspective and join the cult. Most people act like Jehovah's Witnesses about their interests, practically going door-to-door to say, 'Have you heard the word of our lord and saviour, padel tennis?' But with football, there's a certain pain tax you have to pay in order to be accepted into the fray. When someone appears from nowhere, St George's Cross freshly painted on their cheek, label still in their replica shirt and calling him 'Jude Bellamy', there's an overwhelming sense that they haven't been through enough to get here.

The years of humiliation, suffering, boredom, betrayal. Those fucking trumpets at every match. We've *earned* this semi-final; you've just turned up for a selfie on the pitch like Salt Bae in 2022, and you'll be no doubt lifting the trophy in your shin pads despite not even playing, like John Terry in 2012. Much like older generations getting angry at younger people who complain about gas prices, while they had to make do with 'wearing three jumpers' and 'imagining a bowl of porridge', football fans are quick to show the same exasperation. 'These new fans expect the world,' they moan. 'In my day we made do with Darius Vassell, and were happy if we made the round of sixteen.'

Thankfully, England remain a failure. Sure, the past decade may have raised expectations, but that merely makes the disappointment more crushing when it inevitably comes. So I welcome our latecomer fans, safe in the knowledge they're not crashing a party that's lasting much longer. If you only get into football during the tail end of international tournaments to follow England, you are micro-dosing heartbreak.

During international tournaments, Daphne will emerge on match day in one of my old football shirts, making rash statements about tactics she barely understands, effectively cosplaying as me. She has no interest in football any other time, but these brief cameo appearances into fandom have helped her understand what is going on inside my brain any given weekend. Sure, she doesn't have the stomach to follow Spurs and take on this burden of misery year round, but the biennial camaraderie of England appeals to her, and I like having her there for it. Years ago, a small part of me would've hoped we'd stay trophy-less, purely so that latecomers like her couldn't swan in and collect all the free joy. That was until I got extremely into the Lionesses during the same tournament as everyone else and did exactly that. Now I applaud anyone who manages to cut out the thirty years of admin I've been through to get here.

Emotionally investing in England men and Tottenham Hotspur is an absolute dead end, and suits my personality down to the ground. Far from the extroverted tiki-taka style of serial winners like Man City or Real Madrid, not quite the hoof-it-long, hit-and-hope bulldozers of your Stokes and Burnleys of old, but trading on a promise that never quite delivers, with the inevitability of 'nearly' running through their veins. It's said that the worst type of team to support is one that's almost good. If you support an out-and-out great side, your frequent successes more than make up for the occasional stunning humiliations, and if you support a rubbish one, your expectations are so low, even the small positives can elicit huge highs. Drop down to the lower leagues and you even get to trade on the charms of being in it for all the right reasons, being part of an actual community, and really cheap pints. But the *nearly* good sides, burdened by their own potential, never to deliver upon it? That multiplies the shame tenfold.

With Spurs and England, it's always 'gonna be our year', until suddenly it isn't. We get far enough in competitions to start to believe, only to find out we've been gaslit by desire yet again. Spurs have, for the best part of my life, been strongly associated with the term 'bottlers' – famous for snatching defeat from the jaws of victory. I can quibble over specific examples until the football comes home, but ultimately, it's true. Every season we tell ourselves maybe this time is different? Maybe this time we've learned? But I've watched Tottenham change the manager and the entire squad tens of times over the past thirty years and yet still we are the exact same team, making the exact same mistakes, on the exact same timeline.

If you look up scandals and controversies of other football teams, you might find stories of match-fixing or financial doping. If you look the same thing up for Tottenham, you'll find something called 'lasagne-gate', the most Spurs story in history. It was 2006, and needing to win against rivals West Ham to secure qualification to the Champions League, the entire team came down with a bout of food poisoning from a dodgy lasagne at the London Marriott hotel. The game went ahead, and an incredibly washed-out-looking group of players who'd been up all night vomiting lost 2–1, conceding the Champions League spot to their arch-nemesis Arsenal. Is there anything more Tottenham than that? In a do-or-die moment, we literally shat the bed.

Tottenham's own motto is *Audere est Facere*, which is Latin for 'to dare is to do'. Do you realise how sad that is for a sports team? Serial winners would probably argue that To Do Is to Do, but we're happy to just Dare. Our motto might as well be, 'Well, we tried.' And that's what hurts the most. We do it to ourselves. It's who we are.

It's who *I* am, frankly. I've figured out by now I am not one of life's winners. I played football for several low-level recreational teams throughout my childhood, and all I ever cared about was getting out of the games scot-free, unable to have the blame for our defeats placed solely on my shoulders. I feigned injuries to get out of potential penalty shoot-outs and found myself asking, 'How long, ref?' in the twenty-ninth minute. When I play tennis with a friend now, I mentally check out once I've got four games under my belt, knowing that 6–4 is the tipping point at which losing is no longer embarrassing. I hold the record for the biggest victory ever thrown away on *Richard Osman's House of Games*, only needing to finish third on Double Points Friday to guarantee the trophy. It's no coincidence that three decades following my beloved Spurs and England seeped into my body that afternoon to cause one of TV quizzing's greatest ever capitulations. And it hurt. Just as much as the Champions League final in 2019, the 'Battle of the Bridge' in 2017, the league cup in 2021, 2015 and 2009, the Euros penalty shoot-out, Perišić's World Cup goal in 2018, Spain's winner in 2024, Chelsea voiding our Champions League qualification, Harry Kane's penalty miss against France, all of it. I *am* Spurs. And they are me. I wore all of that pain in my facial expression as Isy Suttie lifted the trophy right next to me, moping so much that one of our nation's greatest ever competitors, Dame Denise Lewis, quietly turned to me to say: 'Rhys, it's just a game.'

But it isn't just a game. None of it is. Supporting a football team isn't just checking in on their results, or even watching them play. After a while, it's literally not even supporting them. A football team becomes a part of you. It is your identity. And it's a shortcut to explain to other people who you are. This is a fact I think most football fans would acknowledge. Which is why it's so frustrating when people are dismissive of other people's identity shortcuts. Is a Chelsea badge in someone's profile picture really so different to a Pride flag in another? It's all information. One is telling you this person supports Chelsea Football Club, the other is telling you this person supports The Arts. Is 'Gooner' in a social media bio asking any more of you than 'they/them'? People are so quick to suggest someone might get offended if you called them the wrong pronouns, as though they wouldn't freak out if you suggested, 'You strike me as a Spurs fan.' At least a Pride flag is an act of resistance. What is an Arsenal badge on your profile picture resistance against? Logic? Class? And even the apolitical can be a shortcut to who you are, like identifying as a Capricorn, or a Swiftie. We're all just looking for leadership. For something to follow. Now that most of society has sacked off God, what are we left with, if not some twenty-year-old millionaires who cut holes in their socks, or an American singer who grew up on a Christmas tree farm? Or even some made-up bollocks about the stars themselves? At least Taylor Swift fans actually like her work. I've hated most of Tottenham's output, and yet there I am every week, dressed up like the players, throwing baseless hope into the abyss, watching my dad c-bomb the ref.

In 2023, I went to watch Harry Styles in concert at Wembley Stadium, and as I got to my seat, I realised it was almost the exact same one I sat in to watch England beat Germany in the Euro 2021 round of 16. At the Styles gig, I was taken aback by quite how free his young fans felt to express themselves without judgement. They all wore outlandish outfits, danced without a care in the world, and during one of the slower songs, let off helium-filled heart balloons and lay on the floor to watch them float away. When I was fifteen I wore my mum's blazer to a house party and when a boy called Jake noticed the buttons were on the female side, everyone called me 'Ally McBeal' for the next six months. I couldn't complain: I finally had a nickname I hadn't started myself. Watching my friend's band play at a poorly attended local festival when I was seventeen, I attempted to drum up support by dancing right up at the front. That night, two people from my school posted public MySpace bulletins announcing that I 'danced like dickhead'.

I don't know if it's the bold mentality of the younger generation, whose interrogation of their own identities lets them take ownership of them wholeheartedly, or something Harry Styles himself has cultivated with his own brave wardrobe choices. All I know is I was so jealous in Wembley that night, watching these kids be who they really were in the grateful presence of their hero. I was also incredibly jealous of Harry Styles's body and spent the next three weeks following a diet and workout plan I found in a probably inaccurate *Hollywood Reporter* article about his regime. There was no jealousy during the England match as I watched furious men with their own nicknames on the back of England shirts scream at their own team to do better. One particularly irate gentleman who went by 'Goose' demanded that we take off our greatest ever goal-scorer because he's 'shite'. Twenty minutes later Goose was jumping around in pure ecstasy as Harry Kane scored the goal that put us through to the quarters. If it's impossible to justify what you like, it's also quite hard to explain the way you like it. We're all dressing like our heroes, but some of us are doing it more toxically than others. Either way, whenever I sit in that particular seat at Wembley Stadium, a 28-year-old called Harry makes my dreams come true.

When you leave Wembley Stadium, you join an enormous queue of circa 90,000 people trying to get into the same tube station. It's probably 100 people wide and goes back for hundreds of metres, with the crowd flow controlled by four police horses that turn sideways like gates. Britain is a mad country. After the Harry Styles gig, I listened as people doing this for the first time complained about how long it took. Wembley is already in the middle of nowhere and takes for ever to get home from even if you live a few stops away, which no one does. The queue more than doubles the journey time. But as I heard people moaning, having had the greatest night of their lives, I immediately became those boomers who compared it to how things were in 'their day'. Yes, this queue is long and arduous, but you're doing it after a positive experience. Do you know how many times I've stood in this queue after having my heart ripped out by my own football team? How many times I've stood here, on the wrong side of a knife edge between pride and shame? This isn't a queue, it's an after-party. The real Wembley queue is the one in defeat. Imagine you're standing in it having just watched Harry Styles lose a final on penalties to Justin Bieber, then I'll accept your moaning. Until then, it's as it was.

What all this teaches me is that football, like life, is about moments. I've never subscribed to the idea that unless you win a trophy it was all for nothing. To me, that's always felt like an overly results-based approach to experiences. Your memories aren't null and void just because you didn't get a Wikipedia update afterwards. When I look back, it isn't the pain and embarrassment of football I remember the most, but the brief spells of euphoria. I remember when Harry Kane curled one in from an impossible angle against Arsenal and ripped off his protective nose mask in celebration. I remember when Ollie Watkins took his shot early in the dying moments of the Euros semi-final to stun the Netherlands. I remember when Lucas Moura pulled off a miracle comeback hat-trick to send us through to a Champions League final with practically the last kick of the game. When I think about each of those moments, I feel a rush of adrenaline through my body all over again. When I consider what happened next, I feel no pain or regret. I feel nothing. The latter doesn't cancel out the former one bit.

I returned to *Richard Osman's House of Games* in 2025

for a mockingly titled 'Champions Week', and for the first few days, a similar narrative played out. I flew out of the traps with three easy wins, but as Richard pointed out to my opponents, this is what I do, and capitulation was waiting round the corner. Losing my winning streak on the Thursday, it started to feel inevitable that it was all going to come crashing down again – that I was going to break my own 'Biggest Bottling' record. This time, however, instead of goading myself in the dressing-room mirror like I was in *8 Mile*, I accepted it. I accepted who I am. If this was to be my legacy, then so be it. Let the Reddit statisticians have at it, and bring me back for 'Bottlers Week', see if I don't throw that away as well. As the Friday record came to a close and I claimed my gold trophy, I knew that knowledge hadn't won it for me, but that very acceptance. It was all down to honesty and authenticity. Plus a couple of scrappy 'Answer Smash' tap-ins laid on for me by Simon Rimmer.

Fast forward a few months, and Spurs, too, had their 'Champions Week' to contend with. The final of the UEFA Europa League, a second-tier tournament for teams in Europe who hadn't quite won their respective leagues, but had done relatively well in them. It was very relatable.

When Spurs reached the Champions League final six years earlier, I watched at a wedding. A TV had been wheeled into a back room away from the festivities on my insistence, where I sat in silence for two hours next to a celebrating Liverpool fan. There must have been some small part of me that hoped we'd lose that match, purely so that wasn't my story of victory for evermore: celebrating alone in a hotel function room with a Spurs tie round my head. But now I'd been given a second chance with the Europa League, I found myself in Bilbao with my dad, watching from behind the goal.

I'm not sure if it's because I'd already tasted success with that second roll of the Osman dice, or because we were joined by such infectious optimists in my friends and fellow comedians Chloe Radcliffe and Stuart Laws. I'm not sure if it's because our own manager, Ange Postecoglou, had promised in a post-match interview eight months prior that he *'always* wins things in (his) second year'. I don't even know if it's because earlier that day we had all instinctively popped into a cathedral to pray to a God we didn't believe in. But for the first time in my life, I knew we were going to win – a conviction which bolstered my nervous dad. Our roles were now fully reversed. When we left the cathedral I asked my dad what he'd prayed for. '3–1,' he deadpanned, unable to anticipate a clean sheet in even his most desperate begs to the big man.

But as Brennan Johnson bundled in the worst quality goal, in the worst quality final in living memory, and Micky van de Ven launched himself into the air to block a certain equaliser off the line, it started to feel like the sort of night even a thousand off lasagnes couldn't ruin. For the first time in my life, my faith had been justified.

We had last won a trophy in 2008, when I was seventeen. I had to live my entire life again to see it repeated. Seventeen years of hurt. Seventeen years of *nearly*. But finally, it actually was our year. I had witnessed history. And I was lucky enough to do it next to my father, the man who started it all. The final whistle blew like a pressure valve being released and we gripped each other tighter than ever before, the relief coming off us like steam.

I never believed 'it was all for nothing' when we didn't win. But my God did it feel special when it actually was for something. It didn't matter that it was scrappy and out of character. It didn't matter that we'd been so terrible all season. It didn't even matter that it was only the Europa League. All that mattered was that feeling. In that moment. We had been overpaying the pain tax for years; frankly, we deserved the rebate.

It's easy to be cynical. It's easy to dwell on how things might've gone differently in life. But you can't do it for ever or you'll never move forward. What if Harry Kane scored that penalty against France in 2022? What if we'd beaten Chelsea at the Battle of the Bridge in 2017? What if the ref hadn't been such a cunt in the first minute of the Champions League final? Then maybe it wouldn't have felt so sweet when it finally happened in Bilbao.

What if I'd gone to Borneo when I was seventeen? What if I had been brave when it mattered? What if I had dared to do? Who cares? The new season is starting and you're getting left behind.

You can't spend your life dwelling on all the 'what might've beens' when there's still 'what might bes' to contend with. At some point, it's simply worth more to believe in something, even if you know it's stupid to do so. I didn't realise it at the time, but that's what my dad was really giving me for Christmas in 2001. Not merely a booklet of tickets, but the gift of belief. The courage to trust in something that has given you no reason to do so, in the blind hope it might one day come good. I guess that's why it needed such a big box.

The World Is My Oyster Card

When I was a single man, I had the very cliché habit of falling in love on trains. I operated mostly in the 'stolen glances' you read about, forever waiting for the latest subject of my infatuation to nervously tuck their hair behind their ear and look bashfully into my eyes like the Debby Ryan meme, while I envisaged our entire future together. These days, there are adverts on the tube highlighting various forms of harassment, from cat-calling and unwanted touching to upskirting and staring. Arguably they should go a step further and start policing 'imagining', the creepiest of the lot.

To clarify, my methods were never sexual, nor harassing. In fact, I was probably making such a point of *not* staring that it looked even more threatening, like I was a suicide bomber who didn't want to look into the eyes of his soon-to-be victims. Even my imagination was wholesome, almost tediously practical, rather than the sort of fantasising these adverts warn against, which would likely involve owning a trench coat. Had I ever been called out on one of my own flights of fancy, I'd have been able to offer a reassuring clarification there and then. 'It's nothing creepy,' I'd say. 'Only, if we can't get enough driveway space for two cars in London, I wondered if we'd move out to the suburbs or share one runaround. Obviously one with enough mileage to be able to regularly visit your mum in, I'm guessing, Scotland, when she gets ill, but let's cross that bridge when we come to it. There's no use getting ahead of ourselves here. See? Not weird.'

I now live a life as someone who is occasionally stared at on public transport, and not by trench coat wearers. This is not a brag about my own renown. I am someone people find very difficult to place, gazing at me with the confused head tilt of a Labrador. My face is just distinctive enough for people to think they've seen it before, but I'm not famous enough for them to know where. It's an incredibly awkward quirk of low-level notoriety that you often have to reel off your entire CV to someone until you satisfy their version of reality, in a weird multiple choice quiz where all the options are technically correct. If someone hasn't seen *Mock the Week* or *Live at the Apollo*, we're quickly getting into extremely niche stuff even I barely remember. 'E4's *Virtually Famous*? It was hosted by the wheelchair bloke off *Glee*. No, he's not in a wheelchair in real life. I'm not sure that is OK, actually, no. What about Nick Grimshaw's *Sweat the Small Stuff*? Or Channel 5's *Comedy Game Night*? No? Perhaps ITV2's short-lived sketch experiment *@elevenish*, dubbed "the new *11 O'Clock Show*" before it aired, only to be cancelled after one series? Why yes, I was one of the core cast. Thrilled to meet our fan.'

It's never a great feeling having to run through the Rolodex of now cancelled formats I doomed to failure with my presence, to see which was watched by this stranger. Especially as they usually know you as 'one of the comedians' anyway, or from some deep-cut YouTube football content. These days, if someone asks if I'm 'the guy off' a show I haven't been on, but feasibly *could have* been on, I say yes anyway. Chances are, you are thinking of the right person, but the wrong show. I haven't had any of my lies scrutinised by David Mitchell, or begged for an extra point from Greg Davies, no, but it's heartening to know how much better my resumé is in the false memories of the public. I've also, on more than one occasion, taken a photo with someone under the guise of being Nicholas Hoult to save us both the time. As low as that is, it's nowhere near as bad as verbalising your own Wikipedia page only to find out you merely look like someone this person went to school with and they've never even heard of Comedy Central's *Guessable?*.

All this is to say, when someone is staring at me on public transport, I've always felt quite uncomfortable, and that's without having to worry that person is secretly imagining us on holiday together in St Tropez, riding basketed bicycles with impossible posture, and bopping each other's noses with our ice-cream cones. But that's what I was doing in my early twenties. Still that little kid who simply yearned to yearn. And I should be in prison for it.

While most memories of my passing subjects disappeared as quickly as they did up the tube escalator, there's one experience that has lingered with me. Piccadilly Line, 2012, on my way to perform at a comedy club called Storm in Leicester Square. After university, this was my main gig. I'd get £30 for the fifteen-minute middle spot, which is where a promoter would sandwich a newer act between more reliable pros, so as not to spoil the audience's evening if they turned out to be shit. It was such an established club that often big-name celebrity comedians would drop in to try new material or run their sets for TV appearances. Nothing would excite and scare me more than the idea of one of my potential heroes standing around at the back to watch me perform, flicking ash off their cigarettes and saying things like: 'I like this kid, he's got chutzpah.'

But that didn't have to scare me. Like my various train wives, such scenarios only existed in my imagination. Celebrity comics rushed off to try their jokes at other gigs or arrived too late to see a single second of my drivel. Having faced that disappointment, now that I am occasionally the established act on a bill of newcomers, I make sure to never watch a single second of any of those weasels' sets either. Let the disappointment cycle continue.

All this came to a head one Tuesday evening at Storm. I was booked in my usual spot when the show's promoter phoned to tell me Russell Kane wanted to drop in to test material for a big telly thing, but needed to take the middle section. Brett Goldstein was already opening but had to rush off, so I was bumped up to headliner. Daunting to close the show for the first time, but to follow two heavyweights? What was I supposed to do, call in a bomb scare after the second interval? I'd be lying if I said I didn't consider it.

Half an hour later, the phone rang again. Mark Watson had now been added to the line-up. It was turning into quite the evening for fans of white men and nervous energy, I'll tell you that much. Another hour passed and my phone buzzed once more. At this point I started to wonder if these were prank calls and the promoter was hazing me in some way. Perhaps this was the toxic, laddy comedy culture I'd been warned about but was yet to experience first-hand? My entry fee to the fraternity. But no, Jack Whitehall would genuinely be joining the coveted middle section of this bill. The night was shaping up to look like a comedy Benjamin Button. The same comedian growing progressively younger and more inexperienced as the night went on, with a diversity level somewhere between a Reform Party conference and a *Mock the Week* line-up from 2007.

Needless to say, by the time I was due on-stage, I was absolutely shitting myself. But when I got that first laugh for my opening line (I can't help but feel this is going to be like continuing a wank after you've cum. High-brow stuff.) I felt, ironically, like I'd arrived. I had done it. I'd gone toe-to-toe with the big boys and I finally felt like I was one of them. I was going to be a British comedy icon, rich beyond my wildest dreams. The promoter handed me my £30 and I immediately put a deposit down on a six-bedroom town house in Chelsea.

For the most part, my gigs at Storm were without drama. But the journeys to the gigs? Odysseys of imagined heartache. On this occasion as I sat on the Piccadilly Line, you could've told me I was going on immediately after Lenny Bruce, Richard Pryor and Russell Kane again, and I wouldn't have felt any more nauseous than I already did. My stomach was evaporating from within because I had fallen head over heels, once again, for the stranger sat across from me.

I remember nothing specific about her, obviously, and would be insane to describe it here if I did. Chances are, she was of a similar age to me with something quirky about her, like old-fashioned glasses, or a freakish quantity of hair bobbles. The point is, I loved her. Whoever she was. I was in love with her. But unlike all the other would-be TFL lovers of mine, this one seemed like she might love me back because, for the first time, I felt *myself* being stared at. And I hadn't even been on *Sweat the Small Stuff* yet.

For women, being stared at on the tube is a pretty much constant occurrence. The reasons someone's doing it are obvious, and horrible. But as a man, being stared at by a woman, you're forced to run through the list of possible explanations. Is there something on my face? In my teeth?

Am I holding a baby? Do I have a small dog in a bag? Have I pissed myself? Am I bleeding? Are my headphones disconnected and I've been playing this 'how to discreetly stare at women' podcast out loud? Am I accidentally reading a Jordan Peterson book? Do I not realise that I'm world-famous?

I knew that the answer to all of these questions was no, and so there could be only one option. This woman fancied me and was imagining our future together, too. She saw picnics in the park and arguments over Netflix selections. She envisaged trips to exotic places where we got lost but didn't mind. The rocky start I'd have with her dad before winning him round with a quip about 'the Germans' that I didn't really mean or understand. The first time I'd bravely attempt my Donald Trump impression in front of her. It was all there. She was clearly imagining me building IKEA furniture in the loft conversion, and taking her side when she fell out with her sister even though she was in the wrong. She was doing a me.

It's amazing how bipolar the male ego is, that your rationale for someone looking at you can flip from 'I must've pissed myself' to 'it turns out I'm gorgeous' in a split second. But all my years of wistful train journeys had led me to this moment of mutual understanding. Unfortunately I had somehow neglected to consider someone ever doing it back. This was uncharted territory. How could I be so naive? I felt like a fireman who had practised taking the hose off the truck, but never turning it on. Do I tell her I know? That I feel the same? That I actually prefer Soft Terracotta for the downstairs bathroom?

We shared a few silent glances back and forth, both slowly plucking up the courage to turn fantasy into reality, when suddenly she began to lean forward. As she did, I quickly looked off too far in another direction in an attempt at nonchalance, which had the inverse effect of making me seem far *more* conspicuous, like when a cartoon burglar whistles. I braced myself for a tap on the knee, but it never came, as her lean turned into a stand, and she exited the tube at Holborn.

I'd seen this scene before. This is where the music swells, and I leap up, dash through the doors as they beep closed, race to find her through a crowd, and graze her fingers as I hand back the scarf she dropped accidentally on purpose.

But in reality, I did nothing except crane my neck to watch her through the window as she departed. And for a moment, I could've sworn she was doing the same.

It was difficult to think of anything else as I performed my fifteen minutes that night. Scanning the audience in distant hope she misjudged her stop and was at the gig, as I recited on autopilot my pitiful early gags about how HIV is Roman for 'high five', and I want to get a tattoo that says 'No Regerts'. I always felt pathetic saying nothing to the women I fell in love with on the tube, but this time hit harder, as there was a chance my brand-new dream girl might have actually welcomed my advances. I vowed to never let a future of 100 per cent happiness slip away from me again. To seize the day. To take the chance. What's the worst that could happen? She says no? She says, 'No, you creep, I'm calling the police'? Maybe she says, 'No, I saw you get your pants pulled down in Year 9, you fucking loser,' and then punches me in the face and pulls them down again? OK, quite a lot of bad stuff could happen. But a lifetime of bliss wasn't exactly going to come easy.

I left the gig with no idea how it had even gone, skulking off with my hands in my pockets, kicking up leaves performatively. Then, as I rounded the corner to the station, it happened. I saw her again.

I couldn't believe it. Rarely in life do second chances happen at all, let alone immediately. The universe was telling me this was 'the one', that letting her slip through my fingers hours earlier was no match for destiny. I took a deep breath, patted the creases out of my shirt, and walked purposefully towards her. Soon we were close enough to take in each other's scents. Hers, a bouquet. Mine, not piss. A victory for everyone.

I continued until I was close enough to whisper, my mouth dropping open on the in-breath of imminent speech, and then, with the weight of a thousand missed chances on my shoulders, I walked past her into the station, got on the tube and went home.

Nothing. Again. I did nothing. It's what we both did. Our gazes were slightly more suspicious this time, hearts racing with panic more than passion, and the overwhelming sense of an opportunity vanishing for the second time in quick succession. You don't generally get third chances. And I'd only waste them if I did.

The reality is I remember nothing about this person. She exists as a sort of default Facebook profile picture in my memory. A grey silhouette. But I think about this moment often as a fable that explains who I am. Who I always will be. Another example of a time I vowed to change, and then, at the first opportunity to do so, reverted back to form. Another story that slots perfectly into an already bursting folder of memories marked 'Times I Bottled It'.

For a long time, I thought passing up that second chance was foolish. But now I can see that sometimes you have to accept the moment has passed. Maybe if we'd met that second time and I'd told her I regretted staying silent on the tube – how I couldn't let the moment slip away again, all while

clutching at her shoulders and breathlessly muttering, 'Fate' –
she might have found it charming. More likely, though, she'd
have made some polite excuse and forever told her friends the
story of a man-boy who sat near her on a train, suspiciously
avoided her gaze like a nervous terrorist and then stalked her
across London for the rest of the evening.

Was it ever really going to be the same the second time?
Sure, it may have been a mistake not to go for it initially, if
only to see what might've happened, to push myself. But leaving it alone the second time? Genius. It may have been weak,
but at least it wasn't creepy. There's a fine line between being
a pussy and being an arsehole. And that line is me. I am the
gooch.

When Life Gives You Molehills, Make Mountains

It's 4 a.m. and a man is loudly banging on the window of our cabin, repeating the words 'guide' and 'rock'. Thankfully, we're expecting him, as he's the guide we've enlisted to help us climb a small rocky mountain in time to see the sun rise.

It's a relatively modest climb, but lots of the travel guides I read prior to the trip suggested it's much safer to enlist a chaperone when hiking in darkness, so that's what we've done. He has with him a Dora the Explorer backpack, and is impressively dressed in just shorts, a vest and flip-flops, as though this hike is little more than 'taking the bins out' to him. Meanwhile, I spent about a month researching the perfect waterproof hiking trainers for this exact moment.

We have one torch and one iPhone between us to light our path, which begins along a train track, where we desperately try to stay on the wooden slats without rolling our precious ankles. We walk for around half an hour, over a bridge and into the stony hills, during which time it's established our guide can say exactly one sentence in English: 'Slowly walking, madam.' He means this as advice, an alternative to 'be careful', but he walks so quickly while saying it, it comes across as a sort of outdated stag-do insult, making me even more determined not to trip for fear he starts a chant of 'She fell over!'

It really defeats the point of a nature hike, it turns out, to do it in complete darkness. Sure, we'll get to watch the day dawn from the best vantage point in town, but all that means is there's absolutely nothing to enjoy along the way. This must be how it feels to be a breakfast show DJ. Or someone being ushered into a surprise party with their closest friend's hands over their eyes, ready for the big reveal. Except in this case, they've gone far too early and covered my face for the entire walk from the train station. If we'd done this hike in the middle of the day, we'd be looking at tea fields and streams and wildlife, but here, in the dead of night, I'm looking at nothing but my own phone-lit feet, wondering how these shoes cost so much.

Eventually our guide points out an old decrepit sign that says 'Ella Rock', marking the beginning of the official trail. The only problem is, he pointed this sign out to us an hour ago when we arrived here, and again thirty minutes later. It's become patently obvious that we are walking in circles, completely lost, stuck in some weird hike foreplay. What follows this sign is a steep hill I remember from the two times I've already climbed it this morning and Daphne and I exchange glances as we begin the ascent for a third time. At the top of this hill is a pathway leading left, but last time we were here, our guide chose right, where there is no pathway, but a series of branches and bushes to clamber over instead. Crucially, this choice also takes you down. I don't know if you've ever climbed to the top of something before, but 'down' is the one direction you generally can disregard altogether.

I said nothing the previous times, instead choosing to trust the local man who has lived here his whole life and is walking this route in flip-flops, but as I catch my breath at the top of this hill again, I see this guy in a completely new context. No longer is he a man so relaxed by this hike he can do it in flip-flops. He's an idiot who had no idea what he was letting himself in for. He's wearing flip-flops, for fuck's sake.

'Pathway. Route. Up. Up! Top of rock?' I say, while pointing manically, and shining my phone torch on the clearly marked trail. Our guide stares blankly back. I go harder, more passionate, more adamant. 'This way. It must be this way.' I am absolutely certain, but his face doesn't move. I'd tell him, 'I will die on this hill,' but at this stage, that feels like tempting fate. Eventually he interrupts my flapping with some choice words of his own. 'Slowly walking, madam,' he says as he heads down to the right again.

Daphne and I mutter behind his back for ten minutes, deciding whether to cut and run, try and figure it out ourselves, or, preferably, go back to bed. I can't wind up at the bottom of that hill again. Fool me thrice. After half a mile or so, our guide disappears down some steps towards a small wooden home while we wait at the top. He knocks on the door, chatting in Sinhala to the bleary-eyed tenant who answers. Is that what he's been looking for this whole time? A mate's house to knock on to ask if he wants to 'play out'? Part of me expects him to open that Dora backpack and take out some tea towels he's selling, or at least ask this poor homeowner if he's decided who he's voting for yet. But based on the tone of the chat we deduce that he wants something very different from this guy. Pretty soon the sleepy tenant relents and puts on some sandals of his own, heading out of his house as our new leader, to guide all three of us to our destination.

Now we are following a guide we have enlisted at the recommendation of an online guide, who is following a guide he enlisted due to his own failure to guide. We could've saved an extra hour in bed if we'd hired this guide to begin with. But he's not up to the task either, it turns out. It doesn't take long for him to start looking around just as puzzled as the first guy, and as we round the corner to the bottom of the dreaded hill for a fourth time, we cross paths with an elderly man with a walking stick, and our guide's guide stops *him* for directions. A guide guiding our guide asking some other guy for guidance. All to get to a location whose only directions should be 'up'. Daphne and I trudge apprehensively behind this conga line of clueless gurus, the five of us looking like an evolution of man chart if he never actually evolved.

At the top of the hill, we stand at the crossroads we've been to three times before, and the guide guiding our guide's guide opts for the pathway down the left. When our tired tenant has taken us as far as he's willing to go, our original guide opens his backpack, takes out an *Avengers*-themed plastic folder, and hands over some cash. We're on our own from here. Just me, Daphne and our original hapless guide, flip-flopping his way up a path I suggested we take almost an hour ago.

Soon the trail runs out and we're climbing up slippery rock streams full of leeches and interwoven tree roots. We don't need our torches any more, now half-lit by the soft glint of day slowly creeping in. Daphne and I share a moment of relief as we switch off our phone lights, before realising our ticking clock has just got a bit more urgent. The sunrise we bothered doing this for is imminent.

We start climbing more frantically, but in our haste, Daphne loses a contact lens to the wind, and with it her depth perception. And grip on reality, as she starts to cry at how overwhelming this whole thing is. I grab her by the shoulders, gesture for our 'guide' to fuck off for a second, and summon the memory of every inspirational speech I've ever heard in a film, every half-time team talk I've seen in a sports documentary and even some of the motivational phrases I've rolled my eyes at on Instagram. I know what it's like to be lost in the dark, I tell her. But we've come this far. We can't turn back now, or this has all been for nothing. Time is running out. Forget what anyone says about the process. Fuck the journey. It's about the destination. The journey is horrible. But the destination is the top of this fucking mountain. In time for sunrise. You'll like it when you get there.

I take a deep, self-satisfied breath. Daphne frowns. My speech hasn't worked. It doesn't matter that I'm right, and that she agrees with my logic. We're not dealing with logic, and platitudes like this are a load of bollocks to anyone with half a brain. She tells me to shut up and calls me a twat, as if I need reminding why I love her so much.

'OK, fine,' I say, crouching down so I can look up at her bowed head. 'Three words. Slowly. Walking. Madam.'

She laughs. We both do. And then so does our guide. 'Slowly walking, madam,' he repeats, pointing at me proudly, like I've just said 'garlic bread' to Peter Kay. And we all clamber on up the rocks, Daphne and I pushing each other's arses to get to the top.

We reach the peak just in time for the second half of a disappointingly cloudy sunrise. As we round a corner to the small section of flat rocks on the edge of the cliff, a man in a hut demands a tenner before we can go any further. What a world. You get up at 4 a.m. to circle a mountain four times before climbing to the top in pitch black with a blind girlfriend and a brain-dead sherpa and when you finally get there you're charged ten quid for the privilege of looking at the sky.

We tiptoe towards the edge, where already waiting are

about twelve others: a group of friends, a couple of couples and a wild dog. None of them have brought a guide.

As we go to sit down, I pretend to propose for a laugh. Not the time. We take a seat, completely exhausted, and watch as the day wakes up in Sri Lanka.

I have a few regrets in my life. Choosing a stage name that would be hijacked by a Premier League footballer, not doing enough research into who my neighbours were going to be when buying a house, cashing out the Bitcoin I bought in 2016 when it was 10 per cent of its current price, at a marginal loss. Probably the biggest one is not buying cancellation insurance when I booked, for the second time in my life, a flight to Borneo I was clearly never going to get on. I guess it really is the things you don't do that you regret the most.

As the day of my flight approached, I started to feel a familiar sense of apprehension. Any seeds of doubt in my mind had blossomed into enormous oak trees and I reverted to form, searching for excuses. A single cough would prompt an order of twenty Covid tests; while cooking I'd stare at my kitchen knife, then the tip of my thumb, then back to my knife, fantasising about the damage I might be able to do when inexplicably chopping vegetables seconds before setting off for the airport. When I first told Daphne I had booked the trip, she looked at me exactly like my parents had when I told them I was going to Borneo the first time. Her mouth said, 'Good for you,' but her eyes said, 'Come on, mate, no you're not.'

Or maybe I was projecting. She told me she understood it was something I needed to do for myself, to right a wrong from my past, and apart from some annoying admin around who would look after the cat when she's away for work, fully encouraged my adventure. She even managed to find a cat-sitter, so that excuse was out the window too. But nothing would stop the pit of my stomach bubbling up with dread like always.

I wish there was an actual moment I could tell you about. The scene in a film, where the protagonist sits on a plane, finally going to find that place or that person that will give them closure, until an announcement from the pilot reveals they're going to a completely different destination instead. That they've moved on, they don't need closure. A smile, a sip of inexplicable pre-take-off economy class champagne. End credits. No sign of the fifteen-hour flight they then have to get through, the pockets of open-mouthed sleep, the prick in front reclining his seat right at dinner time, climbing over a neighbour for a piss, drained of any sense of destiny by arrival. But that didn't happen. It just came and went. I suddenly realised I didn't need an excuse not to bother. There was no one to text a hasty fake apology to – I was negotiating with my own brain. It was a plan, and then it wasn't. Time kept passing and I stayed still.

Every now and then I am swept up by moments of complete fantasy, where I plan something ahead, forgetting who I am, expecting to have completely altered my personality by the time it comes around. Cooking and singing lessons, dinner parties with mostly strangers, far-away gigs, all either cancelled at the last second or grimaced through in the hope of yielding at the very least an amusing anecdote, stored in an iPhone note delusionally titled 'Graham Norton'.

But not going on the Borneo trip at seventeen has always meant more to me than chat-show fodder. I have allowed it to define me. To explain me. So to not do it for a second time feels somehow both completely inevitable and absolutely hilarious. Clearly, I am doomed to almost go to Borneo every seventeen years until I'm dead, never learning from my mistakes, just repeating them at greater expense. You won, Emirates, enjoy the money, I hope it makes you happy. Dear lord, what a sad little life.

This time, however, I don't regret bailing out. What would be the point of going to Borneo at thirty-three? I am not who I was at seventeen. It is too late for that experience to be formative. I've been formed. It was probably never a great idea to try to get the monkey off my back by travelling halfway across the world to literally put a monkey on my back. It was never a good idea to try to create a 'happy place' out of a place I've managed to blame for all my unhappiness.

Why not be awake to what's right in front of me instead? What's always been right in front of me. The person I love, who has been shrinking her world to fit mine. And who told me on our first date, twelve years ago, that she's always wanted to go to Sri Lanka, which I ignored to do a bit about Prince Charles fans being nutjobs. I no longer need closure. I've moved on. I moved on years ago, I just didn't realise it. And that's what's known in the business as a 'Chekhov's girlfriend'.

So here we are in Sri Lanka, which, to clarify, was a happy compromise. Sri Lanka is only about four hours closer to home than Borneo and offers a list of very similar attractions. But as I've said before, people love nothing more than to claim something they were going to do anyway was actually altruistic. So I did it all for her.

Our tour is planned out meticulously, with a detailed itinerary designed to pack in as much as possible. Visits to ancient forts and historical monuments, tours of tea plantations and spice gardens, a cultural dance show, waterfall hopping, an elephant safari and even herbal massages, all laid out in a long email from the company we've hired as our escort. Every moment of the day is scheduled, even down to the seemingly unplannable: '16:00–17:00: Relax,' which heaps so much pressure on me it renders itself near impossible. Occasionally one of the activities has the word 'optional' in brackets beside it, as though everything else on this holiday I'm paying for is compulsory. Things like dolphin watching or a lesson in how to thatch a roof from coconut leaves are left to our discretion, but given the chance at a second draft I'd suggest they change it to: 'Sunrise hike – enjoyment (optional).'

This scheduling is not solely down to them, I must admit. At least half of the suggestions come from a cocktail of blogs I've read and regurgitated back and forth in emails over the past fortnight, which Sri Lanka Dream Tours have done their best to accommodate for a self-titled 'little legend'. I have been left to my own devices to select accommodation, and after our culturally enriching daytime plans, we are mostly retiring to fancy hotels and mountainside Airbnbs. There are no tents. No backpacks twice the size of me, like the first day of Year 7. The benefit of doing this trip now that I'm older, aside from the financial, is that I know myself. I no longer have to pretend. I didn't host the Young Pension Awards 2017 to eat from a metal tray in the woods. I am not Bear Grylls. I'm a Booking.com Genius Level 3 member. Half-board, please.

By all accounts, this is the way to go. Everyone told us in advance that the best way to 'do Sri Lanka' was with a driver, and this is such common practice that most hotels have 'drivers' quarters'. I chose to imagine these as hostel-like rooms full of race-car beds, in which the tour guides stay up late, lying on their bellies with their feet in the air, sharing funny tales of their beloved passengers. If only because the word 'quarters' sent a shiver down my spine.

Our driver is Himesh, the jolliest man in the world. He's mid-forties and handsome, smiling cheekily upon greeting us. It's the second time in my life I am met at an airport by a man holding up a sign that says 'Mr Jones', but the first time that it refers to me, and belongs to a driver with a normal-length car. On the transfer from the airport, Himesh delves earnestly into all the current issues in the local political landscape, but just when I start to think all taxi drivers are the same, he interrupts himself to very dramatically inform us that if we'd like him to shut up, he won't speak for the next two weeks. I don't know if it was something in my facial expression that prompted this notion, but the extremely teenage manner in which he does this makes us all laugh. No option to simply move on from the topic – a single shush, and he strops his way into a 300-hour vow of silence.

Apparently most of his passengers choose this option, but it's of no interest to us. We love Himesh already. Every other taxi I've ever been in, I'd have taken the shut-up offer. Or at least politely declined it and spent the rest of the journey in deep regret. But not this one. Himesh is so charming, telling him to be quiet would be like telling a puppy it's not allowed to wag its tail.

Our trip starts on a brief tour of Colombo, an intimidating, sprawling city, where the tuk-tuks are motorised, rather than manually pedalled for £500 a mile, lined with fur and blasting out 'I Gotta Feeling'. Like London though, Colombo is a heady mix of modern metropolis and historical throwback. We visit the Red Mosque, Jami Ul-Alfar, a big beautiful building made up of alternating red and white bricks that takes your breath away, but sits terraced on a street of button shops, T-Mobiles and perfume stalls. Just like in England, where the oak timbers of Stratford-upon-Avon's Tudor buildings are now interrupted by a Robert Dyas sign, and London, where the 900-year-old Tower of London is chanting-distance from a Slug & Lettuce, and Big Ben's clockface overlooks The Shrek Experience.

People find all this sad, but there's something so exciting to me about seeing the old and the new so adjacent. To be reminded that places, like people, are not just one thing. It's possible to adapt without losing your whole identity.

As you walk down the street and let the Red Mosque slowly reveal itself, it feels like seeing an A-list celebrity in your local pub. 'But what are you doing here,' you almost hear, 'in the same place as us? When you're gorgeous. And we're just button shops.'

We leave Colombo after only twelve hours and begin the long drive inland to tick off our list of activities, during which we discover Himesh is obsessed with riddles. Every day when we get in the car he says something like, 'What gets wetter the more it dries?' Or more convoluted ones that start with, 'Three tigers go for a picnic . . .' It suddenly starts to make sense why so many of his passengers from Russia and Germany request silence, but with us, he has met his match. Every Christmas, until I grew too old to have one, my stocking would include a tiny pocket-sized book of riddles and optical illusions, and I would read them all obsessively, trying to come up with my own. On our longer journeys, we go back and forth with different puzzles, some of which I've revised the night before to present back to the group, sometimes accidentally revealing the twists by asking questions in advance like, 'Do you have Monopoly here? How about female doctors?'

As we drive towards Habarana, a small city in the centre
of Sri Lanka which is home to some of the more popular safa-
ris, Himesh starts one with: 'There's an elephant walking
down the road.' How good is this guy, I think, that he can
theme his riddles for each individual stop? I stare at him,
eagerly awaiting the next part of the story, before he points
out that, no, there is literally an elephant in the road fifty
yards ahead of us, walking directly towards the car. It pauses
for a second before sidling past the window to pull down a
branch with its trunk. The moment is so magical I almost
forget how smug I felt thirty seconds ago, when I was about
to humour Himesh with some feigned confusion before
answering: 'The elephant's name is Friday.'

Whenever we're travelling during lunchtime, Himesh suggests we stop off at a Burger King, or if we're outside of a
town, an Americanised hut called something like 'Buddy Boy
Beef Town'. I hope this is a reflection of his previous passengers, rather than what he sees when he looks at us, but we tell
him we want the authentic Sri Lankan experience and to take
us somewhere he would eat if he were driving alone. For the
most part, these are incredible buffets made up of mango and
chicken curries, coconut sambol, dhals, breadfruit and milk
rice. After we've got a taste for it, he takes us into a small village in which an elderly local woman teaches us and some
other tourists how to cook all the aforementioned delicacies,
letting us take it in turns to use a giant six-foot pestle in a
regular-sized mortar. The moment we begin, the heavens
open and flood the paddy fields around us and the damp clay
benches dye us all orange, making us look more Western
than ever. After a valiant group cookery effort, our host dis-
cards everything any of us have done to make all the dishes
again from scratch, and it's here we discover that Himesh has

been dining from a secret hidden buffet behind our tourist ones all along, which houses all the same dishes with increased spice levels. It's the ultimate betrayal, which he finds hilarious. I protest this injustice. Doesn't he know I can handle it? That spice means nothing to me? That I am not afraid of new things? I've done *drugs*, thank you very much, and I once won a prize for trying shepherd's pie.

We head to Ella, a small town in the Sri Lankan highlands, on a train journey famous for its stunning views, reminiscent of a scene from *The Hobbit*, or a desktop background on Windows XP. It feels like I'm seeing the world in 4K for the first time. Daphne and I squabble over the window seat for an hour or so, high on adrenaline from gazing. We have four hours of this ahead, where Himesh will meet us at our destination and take us to the mountain cabin we're staying in, but after ninety minutes slowly tumbling through heaven, Daphne realises we have been going the exact wrong direction. Phoning Himesh, it's confirmed this was due to unannounced platform changes in the rush to get window seats, and while panicking about finding our way back without Wi-Fi or a translator, I am warmed that rail incompetence proves Britain's influence still looms large over the former colonies.

As we disembark in an extremely unwelcoming station, a policeman shouts at me, attempting to fine me for having the wrong ticket. I try to explain the situation, but he can't understand me. Mainly because I am not speaking in comprehensible sentences, but vague French noises and occasional GCSE-level vocabulary about swimming pools and libraries. He says a word I know from Himesh to mean 'idiot' and walks off. *Je ne regrette rien.*

It turns out, in Sri Lanka, there are tourist-friendly trains, and then there are just trains. We effectively got on the rush-hour train from Grimsby to Swindon, and our presence as pale thirty-somethings with a film camera and a Stanley cup is, to put it generously, a 'surprise' to many of the other passengers. To begin with, it's a jaunt back through the scenery from the prior leg of the journey, but somehow it feels more rural, as this time, children wave at us from tea fields and chase the train in the hopes of high fives. Pretty soon though, it's pitch black outside, and for the regular passengers aboard this everyday train, the only thing worth staring at is us. From all angles, we feel eyes on us, in glares that never let up for a second, but this time I don't need to rifle through a list of possible reasons it's happening. I'd say there's a pretty good chance none of these people have seen Series 15 Episode 3 of *A League of Their Own*, and even if they had, I was about as vocal on that as I'm being now. I tell Daphne to act like we belong, pretend we've been working in Sri Lanka for a year and this is our daily commuter train. She looks at me like I'm insane and says, 'Sir, please leave me alone.' That's a bit too method, if you ask me.

When Himesh collects us, he offers us some chocolate by way of needless apology. I take a bite, when immediately I have to stifle a cough at the sharp flavour so as not to seem rude. When he takes a piece for himself a few minutes later, his eyes instantly widen, and reaching for the packet he notices he has accidentally bought Chili Chocolate. Completely baffled, he asks why I didn't say anything, but after all my bluster earlier, how could I? I claimed I could dance with the devil, eat like a local, and now I find chocolate too spicy? I would've taken it to my grave.

Finally reaching our cabin several hours later than planned, we head straight to bed. We're booked in for a sunrise hike up a mountain early in the morning, and after our semi-traumatising train fiasco, we console ourselves with the fact tomorrow will be much simpler. After all, we've booked a guide.

It's been an hour since we got here, and the lazy late risers are starting to turn up at the top of the rock. They say things like, 'That must've been nice, getting here for sunrise!' They have no idea. We dismiss our flip-flopped escort and opt to make the next leg of our journey alone. We're heading to a brand-new temple, pre-opening, on the last-minute recommendation of the family housing us for the next few days, who are besties with the head monk. The pathway is clearly marked, Daphne has managed to find some spare contact lenses in the bottom of her grown-up backpack, and no one's calling me a slow-walking girl. Things are starting to look up.

The temple is breathtaking, with its cupola poking through the clouds like in a fairy tale. Like all religious buildings we've visited, we take our shoes off before entering. Taking my shoes off in public always feels innately childlike. It reminds me of hastily readying myself for a bouncy castle, faking an injury to get out of dancing with a stranger at a Greek wedding, or the dread of a trip to Clarks to get my school plimsolls, or worse, the Cica trainers I was reduced to wearing until I was fourteen due to my feet being too flat for Nike or Adidas. At least there was the measuring machine, and not the fancy digital one you stood on like middle-aged women being conned into learning their BMI in Boots, but the analogue device with the slider that rested on your toes before a silk ribbon was slid down your dorsal and gently tightened. What I wouldn't give to feel that oddly intimate sensation again. For something so sensual it's a disgrace the next thing you were asked to do was stand up and walk around. And moments after a grown-up has pressed their thumb into the front of the shoe and told me I have 'room to grow'? I'm not sure I do, madam, but thank you. What a rush.

As an adult, taking your shoes off while out in the world is admin. Airport security, switching footwear for a commute, removing dog muck with a key. The fun is gone. But it's hard to deny that when you do find yourself shoeless in public, you slow down. Doing it here, I was more careful with my steps, I took more in, and felt more connected to the present. Apparently, we're asked to remove shoes at religious buildings due to respect and sanctity, but I think it's for vulnerability. Without your shoes, you're a kid again, and you're going to need someone to look after you.

This is one of the many tricks of religion. Catholicism traps you with guilt and a desperate bid for approval from the Big Man. Judaism does the same, but with approval from your own mother. Scientology basically threatens to kill you if you even think about leaving. But Buddhism, Islam and Hinduism? Simply take off your shoes and cover your knees. Now you're stuck. Both of those acts simply stop you from being able to run. When was the last time you saw someone win the 100-metre final barefoot in a sarong?

Inside the temple, twenty or so volunteers put the finishing touches on seven enormous Buddha statues, applying gold leaf to his hat, and sanding down his various hand positions. These are called mudras. The Varada mudra, in which the Buddha's open right palm is resting on his right shin, represents charity and compassion. When his hands are together in a praying gesture it means 'offering', and if his index finger and thumb make a circle beneath his waist, it means he gets to punch you in the arm.

With us are couples from Denmark, South Africa and Austria and a lady from Rickmansworth who comes to this part of Sri Lanka every year. The main monk invites us all to take part in some guided meditation, and although the word 'guided' sends shivers down my spine (I can't handle hearing the phrase 'slowly enlightening, madam'), we help carry cushions to the veranda, where we sit in two lines with our legs crossed, mimicking the poses of the Buddha statues inside. With my shoes off, however, I feel more like I'm in a Year 5 assembly, bracing myself to learn about Harvest Festival or the best way to grow cress. Instead, he invites us to close our eyes and leads a chant asking Buddha to free us all from anger, bitterness and jealousy.

In terms of impact, it feels like throwing a coin into a well and asking for a bigger dick. I get the idea. I don't want to feel anger, bitterness and jealousy, but that's the world I live in. A world full of pricks who make me feel all three of those things, often at the same time. Closing my eyes with my legs crossed for twenty minutes a day isn't going to change that, and frankly I feel embarrassed allowing this monk to beg for it on my behalf, like someone who knows the bouncer asking if his mates can come in with him.

I want to be free of jealousy, I do. But the fact this monk seems to be so un-jealous is itself enough to make me envy him. Despite this, I do as I'm told and breathe deeply, and in doing so, consider the fact that so long as this exists, it's a positive. So long as I know it's possible to not feel any of those things, I am not doomed. There is hope.

So when, minutes later, he asks for a five-star review on Tripadvisor, I completely spiral.

It's not that he, or the beautiful temple, doesn't deserve five stars. Frankly, they both deserve six. The issue is who's asking. A monk. A head monk. Coveting a five-star review is exactly the kind of desperation that leads to the bitterness, rage and jealousy he's trying to free me from. So to learn he wants approval as much as I do feels like watching a cartoon policeman lock me in a cell and swallow the key. I will never be free. I will never not care. It simply doesn't exist, and I will spend the rest of my life grappling with a fear of rejection before I can bring myself to do anything.

'It'll really help with the numbers when we open,' he says. I bet it will, mate. So you can drag even more unsuspecting hikers into existential crises until one day you come off the veranda after a guided meditation session and one of the other monks asks how it was and you say, 'Boring. I found it boring.'

I don't say any of this, of course. My shoes are off. I never get in arguments barefoot. But as if to confound my break-down, we're then introduced to another monk. A man from Doncaster who is staying at the monastery in exchange for building them a website. Here we go again. Images that don't match, colliding in my brain. 'See it, say it, sorted' echoing in my ears, having just seen 'something that doesn't look right'. Surely this Northern lad is taking advantage of these Bud-dhists. A monastery, with a website? What's next? A rabbi with an OnlyFans? The Dalai Lama with a vape? The main monk is now taking pictures of the other guests on their iPhones and I start to wonder if I ever actually made it to the top of that rock and this isn't all some concussed hallucin-ation. It feels like a dream when you see someone you know but it's not them, but it is. Everything's off. To look at, it's all as magical as I expected when I built this experience up in my mind, but every time anyone speaks, the whole thing melts in my hands like a Salvador Dalí clock.

We chat to the Northern man for a bit and t'monk senses my trepidation. 'I offered them a website after they let me stay here for a while,' he qualifies. 'I felt like more people should hear about this place, it's so wonderful.' Fair enough, I suppose. That's noble, at least. Church collection plates have Apple Pay now, and that's far more depressing. I liked seeing the Red Mosque so close to those internet cafés and I don't mind the Zizzi's next to the Tower of London, so what's the difference? More people *should* hear about this place. It is wonderful.

I consider getting my phone out to open Tripadvisor, before he asks which bit of the guided meditation I liked best, like the main monk had. I make a quip about how they're awfully keen on feedback, you know, given how they're monks and all, and instantly, in the no-nonsense drawl of Karl Pilkington, he all but calls me an idiot, explaining that it's to help us figure out which bit we find useful so we can use it in our own lives, not so the monks can work on their material.

'Wow, I'm so thick,' I say back, and he laughs. It feels good to be honest. To not give in to the urge to save face, pretend I already knew that and claim I was joking.

After an eventful day, we're picked up at the temple by Himesh, ready to drive us for our last few days on the beach. The south coast is where he lives, and it turns out we're staying about an hour or so from his family who he hasn't seen for two weeks. We tell him to go home and meet us on the final day for the drive to the airport, and his reaction tells me those drivers' quarters aren't what I'd pictured.

We spend our beach days snorkelling, turtle-watching, floating on our backs as the sun sets and sitting on sunloungers playing Monopoly Deal. It's almost like a normal holiday.

I consider suggesting a contest to see who can stay in the sea for the longest, but I already know who would win. It's a blissful end to the trip, which would only be improved by the presence of some of our couple friends to enjoy it with, especially as Arsenal already began bottling the league in December, so there'd be plenty to talk about.

Eventually, the final day comes, and as we wheel our luggage towards Himesh's car, he lets out a deep sigh and says, 'OK . . . it's time,' in the same forlorn tone of a mum driving their kid to university. The journey is far more sombre than the previous ones, the car much quieter, Himesh driving much slower, as if to soak up every last second. When I ask about his work plans after we leave, he sidesteps the question, as if he's dreading ever doing it again.

His birthday is next week, and as we arrive at the airport we hand him a birthday card. Inside, we've written a poetic riddle to which he is the answer. He cries, hugging us both tight, and within seconds, we're both crying too, all huddled together outside Colombo airport, exactly where we started.

When we arrive back at Heathrow, we load our luggage into the back of an Uber. It's an hour or so trip, during which our driver doesn't say a word. Once home and wheeling our bags to the door, my phone buzzes, prompting me to give our driver a rating. I mindlessly go to tap the fifth star, but I pause for a second, stopping myself from giving it away so easily. Before I can decide, I get a text from Fred asking if I want to go for a drink.

'Don't fancy it tonight,' I reply, heading inside.

I'd love to see him. I'd love to do lots of things, actually. But I'll allow myself the night after a holiday to relax before trying to become a new person. 'Maybe next week?' I text back.

We unpack, order a takeaway and I stare at Daphne as she strokes the cat. I feel completely content. Ten minutes later, next door's smoke alarm goes off and it's the loudest noise in the world.

Acknowledgements

It would be remiss of me not to begin these acknowledgements by acknowledging the many other acknowledgement sections I read in advance of writing this one to see what the hell they're all about. Turns out they're like award speeches from people who haven't actually won anything. Which if you've read this far, you'll know is pretty much what I'm all about.

So, first and foremost, to Gareth Bale. Thanks for the memories.

To the people without whom this book wouldn't exist. Zoe Ross, who took a single sentence I said about dread over a coffee and sculpted it into a tangible idea, and whose early notes convinced me I was on to something. Everyone at Wildfire, but notably Philip Connor, who fielded some incredibly basic questions about what a book is, bolstered my conviction in what this one could be, and whose joke tags are dotted throughout this text.

Thanks to Lucas Moura, of course, for those three goals in Amsterdam.

To my mum, thanks for the book title, and thanks for meaning it. I'll be forever indebted to you for your encouragement and protection. No one has conversations like we do. I cherish them. And I cherish how safe I feel to say anything in them. It's a rare thing, and I thank you.

My dad, who famously once said on the radio that he 'thinks about writing a book literally every month'. Your support has always been unwavering but the pep talks you have reserved for specific, crucial moments are the reason I'm still doing all this. I am forever grateful of the environment you both created for us.

Sam. When I was writing this, that duo above kept banging on about how half the book must be about you, given how scared you were growing up. But you never seemed scared to me. Instead, you allayed lots of my own fears. So, thank you for taking your role as big brother seriously. And remember, I will kill ya.

Harry Kane. You brought me more moments of joy than almost anyone. Danke.

Nana. Thank you for being 'where I get it from', for cheating for me during every game and for the Golden Grahams.

To Mark, for being my oldest friend in comedy in every sense of the word. For making me feel like I was part of it all from day one, for your invaluable notes on this book and – most importantly – for the mulligans. Adam, for changing how I write, for always indulging my waffle with genuine interest and for your unique perspective on everything I've ever said.

To Mauricio Pochettino. Thanks for a glorious five years.

To Project Rockstar user Geewhiz, who inspired my earliest pursuits of wit and whose forum post I accidentally plagiarised a decade later during 'Scenes We'd Like To See'.

Ricky at Salon 64, who listened to me chat shit about this book for several months in exchange for this bit of free marketing. To Himesh, who still sends me Buddhist memes every day. Today's one says: 'Attitude is a little thing that makes a big difference.' Too right.

Thanks to Son Heung-Min, obviously. For everything.

To Lilly, for putting up with me saying every single idea for this book out loud to you while you tried to do something else. For dragging me out of my comfort zone while simultaneously being it. For showing me how to get Lime bikes. And most of all, for letting us get Tabitha.

To Evie and Stella, who contributed nothing to this process, but who might find it cool to have their names in here if books come back into fashion someday, like vinyl.

Dele Alli, Dimitar Berbatov, Jermain Defoe, Moussa Dembélé, Robbie Keane, Luca Modric, Aaron Lennon, Darren Anderton, Benoît Assou-Ekotto, Jonathan Woodgate. Thanks, lads.

And thanks of course to the Playaz, Brennan, 'Two Table Tuesdays' and three quarters of The Dregs. Thanks to Chris, Liane, Calum, Aiden. Thanks forever to Dexter Harries, Lolly Adefope and Carl Cooper. Shoutout to David Sedaris, Sue Townsend, Jack Handey and Steve Martin. And thanks to the guy who lived in my house before me for building the shed I wrote this in.

Finally, thanks to Ange Postecoglou, for delivering on that famous claim. For giving me that moment. And for inspiring me to be as bold as you when I say this: I *always* win things in my second book.

RAISING READERS
Books Build Bright Futures

Dear Reader,

We'd love your attention for one more page to tell you about the crisis in children's reading, and what we can all do.

Studies have shown that reading for fun is the **single biggest predictor of a child's future success** – more than family circumstance, parents' educational background or income. It improves academic results, mental health, wealth, communication skills and ambition.

The number of children reading for fun is in rapid decline. Young people have a lot of competition for their time, and a worryingly high number do not have a single book at home.

Our business works extensively with schools, libraries and literacy charities, but here are some ways we can all raise more readers:

- Reading to children for just 10 minutes a day makes a difference
- Don't give up if your children aren't regular readers – there will be books for them!
- Visit bookshops and libraries to get recommendations
- Encourage them to listen to audiobooks
- Support school libraries
- Give books as gifts

Thank you for reading.
www.JoinRaisingReaders.com